W9-CRC-631

THE WEAVER'S
Inkle Pattern Directory

ANNE DIXON

INTERWEAVE
interweave.com

Editor Erica Smith
Technical Editor Lynn Tedder
Illustrator Kathie Kelleher
Designer Anne Shannon
Photographer Jack Deutsch
Production Katherine Jackson

Interweave Press LLC
201 East Fourth Street
Loveland, CO 80537
interweave.com

Printed in China by R R Donnelley.

Library of Congress Cataloging-in-Publication
Data

Dixon, Anne, 1939–
  The Weaver's Inkle Pattern Directory : 400 warp-
faced weaves.
     pages cm
  Includes bibliographical references and index.
  ISBN 978-1-59668-647-2 (pbk.)
  1. Inkle weaving--Patterns. I. Title.
  TT848.D55 2012
  746.1'4--dc23
                        2012002086

10 9 8 7 6 5 4 3 2 1

Acknowledgments

My grateful thanks to all those who have encouraged and supported me to become ever more involved in inkle weaving, especially my family, who somehow manage to not become too entangled in multiple lengths of woven bands.

I dedicate this book to Jenny Barling (who introduced me to inkle weaving); the late Vic Edwards, weaving tutor; the late Peter Collingwood; Madelyn van der Hoogt; Nancy Lee Child; Anneliese Bläse; and all others, past and present, who have helped me.

Special thanks must go to the team at Interweave who have shown immense patience during the past few months: Erica Smith, editor; Lynn Tedder, technical editor; Liz Quan, art director; Anne Shannon, designer; Kerry Jackson, production editor; Allison Korleski, acquisitions editor, and Susanne Woods, editorial director—a village banding together.

Contents

Foreword

I met Anne Dixon in the summer of 2008 at the Handweavers Guild of America's Convergence in Tampa, Florida. Representing *Handwoven* and Interweave, I spent my conference days in the Interweave booth greeting readers and contributors. An unimposing woman with a warm smile came into the booth and introduced herself as Anne Dixon, the author of the recently published *The Handweaver's Pattern Directory*. I was thrilled to meet her, having been impressed by the quantity of weave structures and samples in her book, clearly representing the full life's work of a weaver.

She nodded with brief thanks and bent her head to start pulling things out of a bag at her side and placing them on the crowded table where we were writing up subscription receipts. The items were necklaces and bands, some beaded, most highly patterned, some with sentences on them. Every time I'd pick one up in amazement, she'd place another, more wonderful one, next to it. I could not believe that a person who had woven all the samples in the Pattern Directory could possibly have had time to explore anything else. But that's before I knew Anne Dixon.

In 2010, at Convergence in Albuquerque, she piled notebooks on the subscription table in front of me, notebooks full of plastic sleeves holding bands accompanied by the instructions for weaving them—the first stages of the book you hold in your hands. I couldn't wait to show them to the Books Department at Interweave—and as soon as she left the booth, I bought an inkle loom from a nearby vendor. That loom has been waiting for this book.

Inkle looms have been in use for centuries to weave bands and ribbons. They were replaced during the industrial revolution with mechanized band looms. In the 1930s, Mary Meigs Atwater brought inkle looms to the attention of American handweavers, and they have been available to us ever since. A very clear advantage to inkle weaving is its portability: an inkle loom can go with you on vacations; some are small enough for laps and tabletops. I once thought warp-faced plain weave was the inkle loom's typical product. Not so! Anne Dixon has dazzled me with her extravaganza of color, pattern, and texture.

In *The Weaver's Inkle Pattern Directory*, Anne Dixon has taken techniques from all over the world used on all types of looms and adapted them to the inkle loom in addition to reviving patterns and techniques used on inkle looms historically. In no other volume can you find such comprehensive explanations of how to weave and design inkle pieces. Innovations abound: creating letters and designs using pick-up (with especially clear explanations), adding pile and other textures, combining dye techniques, shaping jewelry, and more. The hundreds of photographed patterns are accompanied by easy-to-follow instructions for weaving them. And not only that, she has created a first-ever, easy-to-use system of graphing inkle designs that makes both weaving them and creating your own easy to do.

The Weaver's Inkle Pattern Directory provides a quantum leap in our understanding of the many techniques possible in bandweaving and how to weave them. The only problem for me is going to be choosing which band to weave first.

Madelyn van der Hoogt

Introduction

When I first saw an inkle loom, way back in the 1970s, I was enthralled. Here was an extremely simple framework—no treadles, no levers, no rollers, no ratchets, no shafts—just simple hand movements to raise and lower the warp. And patterns emerged!

My friend Jenny said, "Don't buy one of those, Anne, you'll be bored within three weeks." I heeded her advice for a while, but started trying to find out more. Not a lot of information was available at the time, but there was enough to entice me into disregarding her advice and buying my first inkle loom.

Since those early days, various fellow weavers have introduced me to different concepts. Vic Edwards suggested lettering (no information was available then, so I developed my own method); Anneliese Bläse shared her collection of Baltic-style patterns; Peter Collingwood gave information about the same techniques sometimes appearing in different cultures.

Nearly forty years later I am still excited by the possibilities afforded by weaving with this narrow loom. It is because the inkle loom is so narrow that we are encouraged to push the boundaries beyond those of a basic 2-shaft loom.

No, I am not bored; instead, I'm sometimes overwhelmed by ideas! There are so many evolving ideas and other techniques still to explore fully, but this presents many of the traditions and innovations that link us to the past, present, and future.

Anne Dixon

About This Book

What is an Inkle?

Basically, an inkle is a warp-faced plain-weave band.

Plain weave, or tabby, is when one set of alternate warp threads—those that are on the loom—are raised above the other set of alternate warp threads, and the weft thread is inserted between them in that shed (or opening between warp layers). Alternating the two natural shed positions, by first raising the unheddled threads and then lowering them, creates a tabby or plain-weave structure.

A warp-faced weave is when each layer of the warp threads crowd together both above and below the weft thread, with the weft lying completely straight in the shed. The weft thread is completely covered and does not show except at the selvedges, where it turns to exit one shed and enters the next.

Each of the warp threads is forced into a pathway first over and then under the weft thread. This pathway is curved more than in a balanced weave, where both warp and weft show. The finished length of a warp-faced fabric is considerably less than one of balanced weave.

Structure of the Inkle

This is a weft cross-section showing the path of one warp—red warp thread, yellow weft:

This weft cross-section shows the path of two adjacent warp threads: red and blue warp threads, with yellow weft:

The length of warp thread needed to go around each weft pick is ½ warp thickness + weft thickness + ½ warp thickness (see below).

This means that the length of the pick can never be less than 1 thickness of a warp thread (½ + ½), *plus* the thickness of the weft. If a weft the same thickness as the warp is used, then the length of the pick will be at least twice the width of the yarn. It is usually preferable to use a weft the same thickness and color as the warp-selvedge threads, as then, even at the selvedges, the weft will hardly show. In order for the minimum height of the pick in the warp to be increased twofold, the weft must be nine times as thick as the warp threads: the weft height must be three times the warp diameter, which necessitates a yarn nine times as thick because it becomes compressed when beaten (see below).

Because the warp takes a sinuous pathway over and under the weft, the length of each finished inkle is considerably less than its original warp length. (See page 9 for information about tension devices.)

The width of the inkle is dependent upon both the number of warp threads and their thickness. Only half of the warp threads are on the surface at any one time, and as these threads crowd together, the width of the inkle will be about half the total width of the warp threads wrapped around a ruler. This can only be approximate because the width the warp draws in may vary, and some threads are softer than others. However, a general rule is to wind just under twice as many threads for the warp as are needed to wrap around the chosen width. Experience is the best guide, and even then, sampling before weaving each inkle will establish the accuracy (see page 161).

How to Read the Drafts

Each sample is preceded by the warping draft. This is shown as a two-line chart. (Except for krokbragd: see page 102.)

The colored squares in the upper line of the warping draft are those warp threads that go over the top peg and are then held down by heddles (marked H in the drafts). Colored squares in the second line of the warping draft are those warp threads that pass under the top peg and are left unheddled (marked U on the drafts).

A heddle row is when the heddled threads are in the upper layer (unheddled threads pushed down).

An unheddled row is when the unheddled threads are raised to the upper layer.

This is a typical basic warping draft:

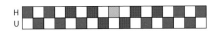

The warp threads are wound by reading from left to right, alternately winding the first thread from the top line (heddled threads, H) and then one from the lower line (unheddled threads, U), and so on along the draft. Below is the same draft with repeat marks for simplification.

Sometimes there are even more repeats containing sections that are themselves repeated.

Here the center section is repeated three times:

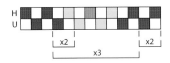

Occasionally some of the warp threads need to be thicker than the others, or perhaps two thinner threads need to be used as one. These are shown by widening the filled square into a rectangle.

These are thicker, or doubled, warp threads in the warping draft:

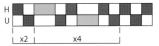

Where necessary, further details about warping drafts for specific techniques are in the explanatory notes preceding the technique sections.

Pattern Charts

With basic warp-color patterns, because the warp layers crowd together, each successive row (or pick) lies indented from the one preceding it, rather than directly beneath.

This is the true appearance of the inkle:

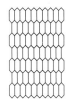

To make it easier to read the pattern charts, but still keeping the ratio of warp thickness to pick length as 1:2, I have devised the indented lengthened grid (below), which gives a good representation of how the woven inkle will look.

Other techniques have their own type of pattern chart. Details about reading the pattern charts for each specific technique are in the explanatory notes preceding each technique section.

Reverses are not shown for basic warp-color patterns, as they are the same on both sides.

The page layouts feature the warping draft at the head of the column. If both columns have the same drafts, then only one is shown.

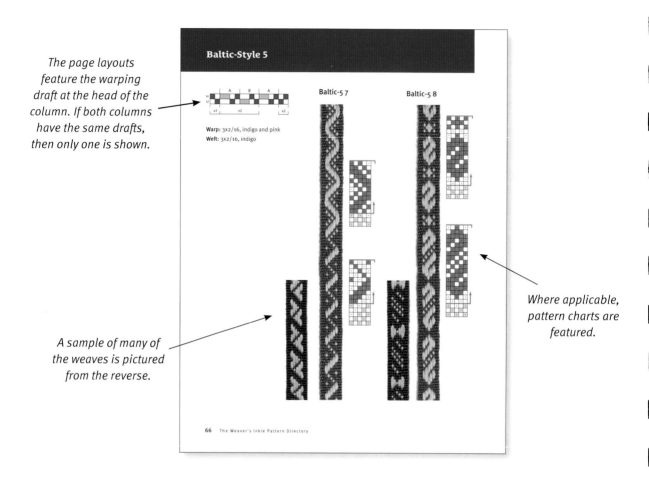

A sample of many of the weaves is pictured from the reverse.

Where applicable, pattern charts are featured.

Modern Inkle Looms

The most common form of inkle loom is the table model, which has pegs fixed into a framework at one side and is open on the other. The open side is generally at the right, but if you have difficulty in using the right-handed variety, you can sometimes obtain a left-handed loom, with the open side at the left.

The inkle loom should be strong—not just the frame—and the pegs also need to be extremely securely fixed. A great deal of tension is placed on the pegs during weaving. If they are too thin, they may break; if they are too long, they may either bend or break; and if they are not fixed into the frame securely, they may break or come out of their holes.

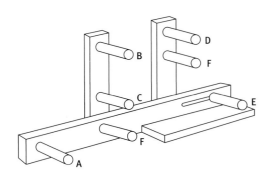

The inkle loom

A. *Starting peg.* This can sometimes be a sliding device for tensioning.

B. *Top peg.*

C. *Heddle peg.*

D. *Joining peg.* This may also be a tensioning flap.

E. *Tensioning device*—either a slider or a flap. This can be positioned anywhere on the loom.

F. *Other pegs* for making a longer warp—these vary in number.

Adjusting the tension

The second important requirement of any inkle loom is that there be some form of tensioning adjuster. The purpose of the tensioner on an inkle loom, regardless of type, is to allow enough extra length on the continuous warp to compensate for the large amount of warp take-up that occurs with warp-faced weaving. (A fixed-length warp would become tighter and tighter as the inkle was woven, finally making it impossible to weave.)

The tensioning adjuster is usually one of two types. Some looms have a sliding peg; others have a swiveling block or flap. Both can work extremely well.

In order for the sliding peg to work best, two pegs need to be opposite to, and a little distance from, the sliding peg, but not on the same alignment as each other. The pathway of the warp around the pegs and tensioning adjuster must be arranged in a continuous loop that never crosses itself; otherwise, it will not be possible to advance the warp around the pegs.

For the swiveling block or flap to work best, the pathway of the warp as it approaches and leaves the flap needs to be at an angle, rather than a straight line. If it is not, the possible adjustment may be very slight.

Heddles

The warp passes from a starting peg to a joining peg (which can sometimes be the tensioning flap). In between, the warp threads go alternately either over or under the top peg. The threads that go over the top peg will have a heddle on them, which will bring the level of the warp down to the level of the threads passing under the top peg. The heddle peg will be almost directly under the top peg.

There are three main types of heddles: a loose single, a fixed single, and a double type. The disadvantage of the single types is that it is necessary to thread the warp yarn through the heddle while warping the loom.

The advantage of the double type is that it is placed on the warp thread after warping and is passed from the heddle peg, over the warp thread, and back to the heddle peg, thus making it possible to warp directly using large balls or cones of yarn.

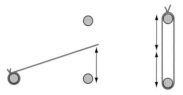

The heddles need to be the right length and all the same size. Looms vary considerably, so to determine the size, tie a thread to the starting peg, take it UNDER the top peg and over the joining peg and down to another peg and secure it (see above left). The distance from the heddle peg upward to the yarn is the length of the heddle.

For double heddles, find two pegs on your inkle loom that are TWICE the distance of the measured length (see above right). Make individual heddles around these two pegs, tying them securely with three knots. If no two pegs are the right distance apart, make a heddle jig by nailing two long nails all the way through a piece of wood so that you can slip the heddles off the nails as they are made.

The advantage of using two pegs on the loom is that they are always available when you need to make new ones. A strong, smooth yarn is best for heddles. Cotton or linen is ideal, as silk or synthetic yarn can sometimes cut into the warp threads. Heddles do get worn with use, so make a few extra each time.

To make a knot when working alone, first tie a single knot against the peg, make a loose second knot above it, and, holding the ends with the thumbs and first fingers, pull the ends until the space between the two knots is just the right size in which to place the third or fourth finger from each hand. Pull the first knot tight with your inserted fingers, slip one finger directly onto the tightened first knot to hold it, then pull the ends to tighten the second knot against the first. A third knot can also be tied on top of this for extra security.

The heddle is placed around the warp thread that goes over the top peg, holding it down while the top peg holds it up, so that the heddled thread is fixed in place.

To put a heddle onto the warp thread, first loop the heddle onto the heddle peg (with the knot underneath), take the loop back and then over the single warp thread, bring the heddle back down to the heddle peg, and place the end of the loop over it—no threading.

Shuttles and beaters

There are so many types of shuttles on the market. Some form of a stick shuttle can be used to hold the weft, but it shouldn't be too long, because then you will spend too much time rewinding the shuttle as you weave.

Shuttle for inkle weaving

Even the smallest shuttle will require rewinding at times. As you weave from side to side, the shuttle will often unwind one length at a time. But a shuttle of just the right length to suit the width of an inkle would be so short as to make it impractical.

Winding a shuttle

When winding the shuttle, take it around the length in a straight path—crossing over at the edges increases the thickness of the wound weft at the center of the shuttle, thus decreasing the availability of space for the weft. Don't wind so much that the shuttle cannot be used comfortably, especially if the shuttle is also used as a beater. It is very simple to join in a new weft thread (see page 15).

The shuttle can itself be used as the beater or a separate beater may be used. (Plastic netting shuttles are usually too weak to use as beaters.) Some people prefer to have the weft yarn loose in a small bundle. This is ideal when weaving short or separate sections with single lengths of yarn.

A beater does not need to be heavy—the beat is more of a strong push (see page 14). Both beater and shuttle could have a beveled edge, but it is not vital.

Shed sticks

Shed sticks are invaluable for starting, making spaces, picking up threads, and marking the width. You will need a minimum of three shed sticks. They need to be thin, narrow, smooth, and not too long. Wooden ice-pop sticks or coffee stirrers are good, but be sure to shorten the length somewhat. Plastic plant markers are good, but perhaps are a little too wide. They can also be marked with a pencil as to the width of the inkle as a handy check during weaving.

Pick-up sticks

Traditionally this is a thin stick, with one point slightly rounded and perhaps curved. A shed stick or short double-ended knitting needles could be used. Most readily available: your fingers. An inkle is, after all, pretty narrow.

Working at the Loom

You will need to find the correct height of chair on which to sit so you are comfortable when weaving. Standing is not recommended. A table-model loom is often best placed on a table that is a little higher than the seat height—sometimes a slightly higher chair can be used, but it is entirely a matter of preference. Floor-standing inkle looms are also available. The main advantage of a floor model is that the total available warp length is often considerably longer than that of a table model.

Weaving Inkles without an Inkle Loom

It is not essential to have an inkle loom to weave inkles, although it does make inkle weaving much easier. An inkle loom is quick to warp, easily portable, has its own tensioning device, and does not tie the weaver to the loom as a backstrap loom does. The modern inkle loom was not devised until the beginning of the eighteenth century and, indeed, the table model not until the beginning of the twentieth century. However, inkles were made for hundreds of years prior to this. The first written record is 1540, and William Shakespeare refers to them three times. Obviously,

they were made on something other than the inkle loom, and these methods can be used or adapted to weave inkles without an inkle loom.

If you're weaving an inkle on a shaft loom, it is best to use a minimum of four shafts, threaded as a straight draw, with shafts 1 and 3 worked together alternately with shafts 2 and 4. Dispense with the reed and beat using the shuttle or flat stick. You could emulate some of the later medieval weavers and weave two or more inkles simultaneously, side by side, each with its own separate shuttle.

Inkles can also be woven on any two-shaft loom or with a rigid heddle (also known as hole-and-slot heddle; see above left). The warp threads are threaded alternately through a hole and then a slot. Lift the rigid heddle to create one shed and push it down to create the second. Remove the reed if you have one, and if you're using a rigid heddle, use it only to open the two different sheds. Do not use it to beat the weft in place. Instead, always use the shuttle or a thin stick.

Although the rigid heddle is more often seen as a handheld tool, in medieval Europe, a standing variety was used (see above right). The heddle was larger and placed on an upright stick or held in a frame so that the holes were at waist height when one was working while seated. To use it, you only need to lift and lower the woven inkle at the fell, and the sheds will open. It was used either with a backstrap arrangement or two fixed points. Many early types of band looms, including the standing rigid heddle, were taken to North America by the Europeans.

Basic Techniques

Warping

Originally the modern inkle loom would have been warped with one continuous single-color thread, alternately passing the warp thread over and then under the top peg and tying the end of the last pass onto the beginning of the warp. The main disadvantage of a single continuous warp is that the warp tends to become tighter with each successive wind, even when heddles are added (or threaded through) during warping.

Sometimes people like to emulate the continuous warping, even when using different colors, either tying on the new color at each change or by wrapping the ends of the warp threads around different nails near the front of the loom, unwrapping to continue with that color when it is next needed, and again when tying all ends to the beginnings of the warp colors.

When several different colors or threads are used for warping, the extra tying on or securing/releasing of each new yarn and the entanglements that can ensue (resulting in crossed threads at the end of the warp), plus additional tensioning problems, hardly justify strict adherence to the original method. The following method seeks to eradicate the disadvantages and is at least as fast as tying in the different threads. Plus it is always easy to see exactly where to place the heddle. (See page 10 for tying a knot by yourself.)

These instructions assume that the first and last warp thread is a heddled thread.

- If the first warp thread is unheddled, start at step 2 (a or b).
- If the last warp thread is unheddled, finish with a single warp thread under the top peg.

1. Warp the first thread over the top peg, along the chosen pathway. Push the thread to the frame of the loom at all points, cut off, and tie securely with two or three knots at the starting peg. Place a heddle over the heddle peg, take the loop behind the warp thread, back down and loop over the heddle peg, with the knots under the peg.

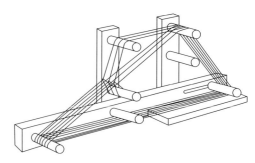

Loom with heddles

2a. If the next two warp threads are the same, first wind one pathway under the top peg and then continue with the next over the top peg. Push both warp threads to the frame of the loom at all points and tie as above. Place a heddle on the last (over peg) warp thread.

2b. If the next two warp threads are different, then hold both threads together and take their correct pathway around the loom, placing the first (unheddled) thread under and the second (heddled) thread over the top peg. Push both warp threads to the frame of the loom at all points and tie together as above. Place a heddle on the last warp thread. If you find that the heddled thread is always too tight, tie the beginnings of the warp threads together and at the finish, place one thread through the loop above the beginning knot, and then tie the ends of the two threads together.

Repeat using either 2a or 2b.

Adding heddles as you go along is far quicker and more accurate. Warping only two threads at a time helps to reduce the tendency for the warp to tighten.

Minimum and maximum length

The warp on any one inkle loom has a possible minimum and maximum length with variations between the two.

The *minimum* length for any warp is from the starting peg, to the joining peg, around the tensioner, and back to the starting peg without interfering with the heddle peg.

The *maximum* length winds zigzag around the tensioner and all the pegs on the loom, without interfering with any of the other pegs or the pathway of the warp.

Yarns to use

Warp yarns need to be strong—they are under a lot of tension on the loom. The easiest yarns to use are smooth; although textured yarn can be used, it's not suitable for a beginner. Far too often it is suggested that first experiments in handspun yarn can be used on the inkle loom—definitely not! Even experienced inkle weavers can have tension and abrasion problems with handspun yarns in the main part of the warp. But handspun can be used if under light tension as in Scribbling (see page 119) or Embroidery (see page 123).

Weft yarns do not come under such tension, and they usually lie completely hidden within the warp, only showing at the edges. To hide even this, the weft is usually the same color as the outer threads of the warp and also the same type and thickness.

Other equipment

Keep scissors, pencil, tape measure, and notebook on hand, possibly stored in a dedicated inkling box.

Two-sided looms

Sometimes you might see looms that have a frame at both sides. These are far more difficult to warp and weave. Better solutions would be a rigid heddle or a 2- or 4-shaft loom with front and back beams.

Weaving and Beating

The heddled threads are held in a fixed position by the top peg above and the heddles below, so they cannot move. Unheddled warp threads have no such restrictions and can be pushed up above and down below the heddled warp threads. This is what creates the shed or space for the weft to be inserted during weaving.

Because there is no mechanism for spacing the warp threads, they crowd together completely hiding the weft thread—this produces a warp-faced fabric.

Position the inkle loom so that the starting peg is next to you, just above your waistline, and the framework is at right angles to you. Place one hand beyond the heddles, below all the unheddled threads, and push upward so that they are above the heddled threads. Next push all the unheddled threads downward so that they lie below the heddled threads. These are the two possible sheds, which, when woven alternately, produce a tabby or plain weave. You can use the same hand each time for these two movements, or opposite hands. Experiment to find which best suits you.

Wind the weft onto the shuttle if you are using one (see page 11). Experiment to see from which direction you prefer to insert the shuttle into either of the two sheds and collect it from the opposite side. Everyone has his or her own preference—none is incorrect if it suits you.

Only after the shed is changed is the weft beaten into place. There is no point in beating the weft until the shed is changed because it will buckle at the sides. The weft must lie completely straight; otherwise the warp threads at the edges will migrate outward and make the selvedges untidy.

The sequence for weaving is:

Change: Open the shed, holding the shed open with the nonshuttle hand.

Beat: More of a hard push. (See page 14.)

Tug: Tug the weft to straighten out the weft that has buckled in the previous pick. (After beating you can leave the shuttle in the shed, probably holding with one hand, while you tug the weft with the other hand.)

Weave: Insert the weft and hold under tension, using both hands, as close to the fell as possible. Gently hold the far edge of the inkle as the weft finally slides into position, ensuring that the warp threads at the weft-entry edge are nudged firmly (not pulled) close together.

Continue weaving in this way—change, beat, tug, weave—inserting the weft first from the right and then from the left.

You will soon establish the sequence of weaving.

For some techniques, you will need to insert the first two fingers of both hands into the shed to manipulate the threads. Details of this, where necessary, are given in the technical notes at the start of the technique.

Beating is more of a firm push against the fell of the inkle (the last part woven). One push should be enough. You can also wriggle the beater (or shuttle) up and down horizontally, holding against the fell, to lift and depress the warp threads even further into position.

You will notice when you do this that the last part of the weft buckles upward through the previous shed—that is why you need to tug slightly. If the weft has been inserted firmly and neatly, then it should not buckle at the opposite edge; if it does, then straighten as necessary.

Starting and Finishing

If the ends of the weft are left loose, then the edges of the inkle will move outward when it is removed from the loom, making the selvedges uneven. So a secure start and finish is advisable.

Open up one of the sheds—it doesn't matter which—and insert a shed stick. Change the shed, push the first shed stick down to the starting peg, and insert a second stick. Repeat so that there are three shed sticks in place. Change the shed once more.

Insert the shuttle through the open shed (from the side that suits you) and leave a tail of the weft hanging at the side. Change the shed, beat, and tug (both edges this time). Weave both the tail and the shuttle into this next shed, then change the shed and continue weaving. The tail of the weft will remain secure and can be trimmed later (see below).

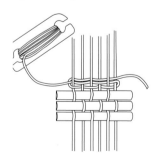

To finish weaving, at the penultimate pick, weave the weft through a shed. Into the SAME pick, insert a loop of smooth thread with the loop at the opposite side to the shuttle.

Change the shed, beat, and tug.

Weave the shuttle through this final pick.

Cut the weft, leaving about 8" (20 cm). Insert the very end of this tail into the loop—not too far—so that it creates a loop clasped with the first.

Now, holding both loops gently in opposite hands, pull the clasped loops through the shed, positioning the upper (final) weft into place, and pulling the weft completely through the previous pick.

Again, change the shed and beat.

Discard the extra loop of thread. The weft will remain secure and can be trimmed later. This saves having to darn the weft into place after the inkle has been cut off the loom, and it is extremely secure (see below).

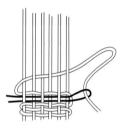

There is no need to secure the ends of the inkle any further when the inkle is removed from the loom, but sometimes a decorative or braided edging is required. Remember to leave enough unwoven warp so that this can be done; generally braiding uses about 1½ times the finished length. (See pages 163–164 for further information.)

Spaces

If you wish to leave a space and start a separate piece on the same warp, first finish the previous inkle as above.

If the space is quite short, insert shed sticks in a weaving sequence for the desired length before starting the next inkle.

If the space is longer, leave the warp unwoven for almost the required distance; insert 3 shed sticks in sequence, as at the start. Start the inkle as previously and continue weaving.

Woven Width

Weave a short sample at the beginning of an inkle if you are not sure of the optimum weaving width. When this is established, mark the width (on a shed stick or piece of paper/card) and keep it by you as you weave. Constantly refer to it during weaving and adjust the pull-in of the weft to suit. (See also page 159.)

Moving the Inkle Around the Loom

When the warp can no longer be manipulated easily, release the tension and slightly ease the woven inkle down to 2" (5 cm) from the starting peg. Tighten the tension, push the heddles back to their position (they will have moved down with the warp threads toward the starting peg), and move all the warp, woven and unwoven, close to the framework of the loom.

The end of the available warp: The knots made at the start will appear over the joining peg. Work as far as possible and finish as described previously.

Slits

An inkle band can be woven as two (or more) separate vertical pieces. Each piece must have its own separate weft thread. The slits can be used as buttonholes, to insert one inkle through another.

Starting at the beginning of the weaving: Just start each part as shown previously, with a separate weft thread for each, and weave the sections simultaneously but separately across the weaving.

Dividing in the middle of weaving: Weave one pick and insert another weft into the same pick at the point of the slit with the tail opposite to the shuttle.

Change the shed, beat, tug.

Work a starting technique with the new weft in that section; weave the first weft into the separate section; change the shed, beat, tug, and continue to weave each section simultaneously using the same picks.

Joining slit pieces together in the weaving: Weave both wefts right across the pick. In the next pick, weave the secondary weft back to the slit point, but continue weaving with the main weft. The tails can be snipped off after the inkle has been taken off the loom.

Joining in a New Weft

When the weft thread is finished, add the start of the new weft in the same pick as the old and in the same direction, leaving a very short tail; subsequent weaving will secure it in place. Snip off the protruding ends neatly when the inkle is complete and off the loom.

Problem Solving

A broken heddle: Make a temporary single heddle: Loop a yarn over the warp thread and tie down to the heddle peg so that the warp thread is at the same position as before.

A broken warp end: Tie in a new warp end along the same pathway (through the heddle if necessary), tying at the starting peg. Continue to weave as usual. When the inkle is removed from the loom, carefully darn in the two loose ends, keeping the direction correct, for a little way, then snip off the extra thread; or hang an auxiliary warp thread, winding the start around a horizontal pin placed back about 1" (2.5 cm) in the woven part of the inkle (see page 110).

The Craftsman's Creed

All of the fine traditions and the skill
are mine to use to raise
my craft renown
and mine to teach again with
reverent will.
Thus do I love to serve,
with fingers that
are masters of the tool.

Pattern Directory

Dots and Bars

Dots and Squares

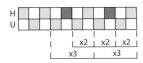

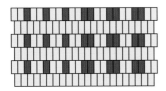

Warp: 3x2/16, dark green and lemon

Weft: 3x2/16, lemon

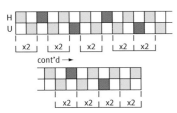

Single dots and 2 adjacent heddled threads for squares.

Bars

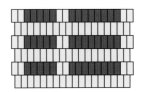

Warp: 3x2/16, dark green and lemon

Weft: 3x2/16, lemon

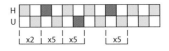

Several adjacent heddled warp threads for bars.

Offset Dots and Squares

cont'd →

Warp: 3x2/16, dark green and lemon

Weft: 3x2/16, lemon

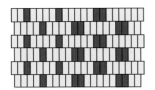

Single dots and 2 adjacent threads both heddled and unheddled.

Offset Bars

Warp: 3x2/16, dark green and lemon

Weft: 3x2/16, lemon

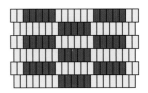

Several adjacent threads both heddled and unheddled.

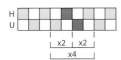

False Checks with 2

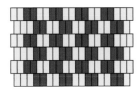

Warp: 3x2/16, dark green and lemon

Weft: 3x2/16, lemon

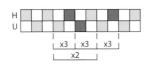

Note that the colors do not form complete squares because each row is indented.

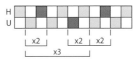

True Checks with 2

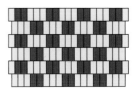

Warp: 3x2/16, dark green and lemon

Weft: 3x2/16, lemon

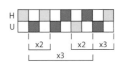

Dark green squares within a lemon background.

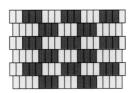

False Checks with 3

Warp: 3x2/16, dark green and lemon

Weft: 3x2/16, lemon

Again, the checks do not form complete squares.

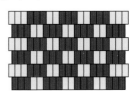

True Checks with 3

Warp: 3x2/16, dark green and lemon

Weft: 3x2/16, lemon

Lemon squares within a dark green background.

Single and Double Stripes

Warp: 3x2/16, dark green and pale blue

Weft: 3x2/16, pale blue

All stripes curve the same way.

Single and Double Stripes in Opposition

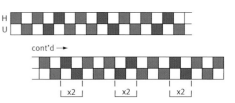

cont'd →

Warp: 3x2/16, dark green and pale blue

Weft: 3x2/16, pale blue

Stripes curve opposite to adjacent stripes.

Triple Stripes

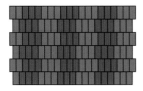

Warp: 3x2/16, dark green and pale blue

Weft: 3x2/16, pale blue

All stripes curve the same way.

Triple Stripes in Opposition

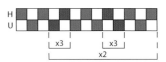

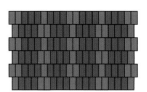

Warp: 3x2/16, dark green and pale blue

Weft: 3x2/16, pale blue

Stripes curve opposite to adjacent stripes.

1:2 and 2:3 Stripes

Warp: 3x2/16, dark green and pale blue

Weft: 3x2/16, pale blue

Uneven stripes curve the same way as the adjacent stripes.

1:2 and 2:3 Stripes in Opposition

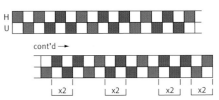

cont'd →

Warp: 3x2/16, dark green and pale blue

Weft: 3x2/16, pale blue

Uneven stripes curve opposite to the adjacent stripes.

3:4 Stripes

Warp: 3x2/16, dark green and pale blue

Weft: 3x2/16, pale blue

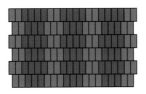

Uneven stripes curve the same way as the adjacent stripes.

3:4 Stripes in Opposition

Warp: 3x2/16, dark green and pale blue

Weft: 3x2/16, pale blue

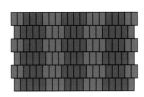

Uneven stripes curve opposite to the adjacent stripes.

Cables & Flowers

Single Cables

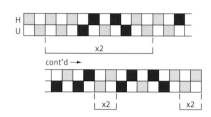

cont'd →

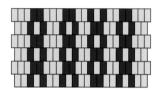

Warp: 3x2/16, dark green and pale green

Weft: 3x2/16, pale green

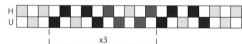

Single Flowers

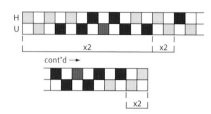

cont'd →

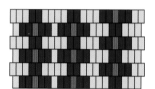

Warp: 3x2/16, dark green, pink, and pale green

Weft: 3x2/16 pale green

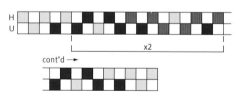

Adjacent Cables

Warp: 3x2/16, dark green, pink, and pale green

Weft: 3x2/16, pale green

Adjacent Flowers

cont'd →

Warp: 3x2/16 dark green, pink, and pale green

Weft: 3x2/16, pale green

Separated Chains with Single Ends

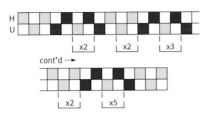

cont'd →

Warp: 3x2/16, dark green and pale green

Weft: 3x2/16, pale green

Separated Chains with Doubled Ends

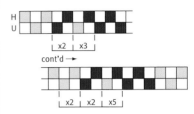

cont'd →

Warp: 3x2/16, dark green and pale green

Weft: 3x2/16, pale green

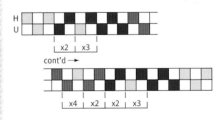

Adjacent Chains with Single Ends

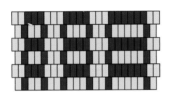

Warp: 3x2/16, dark green, pink, and pale green

Weft: 3x2/16, pale green

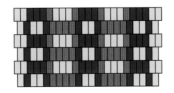

Adjacent Chains with Doubled Ends

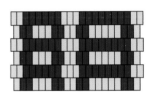

cont'd →

Warp: 3x2/16, dark green, pink, and pale green

Weft: 3x2/16, pale green

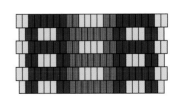

Zigzags (Offset Bars)

Even-length Alternating Bars

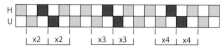

Warp: 3x2/16, dark green and mauve

Weft: 3x2/16, mauve

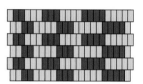

Even-length Overlapping Bars

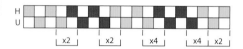

Warp: 3x2/16, dark green and mauve

Weft: 3x2/16, mauve

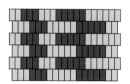

Uneven-length Alternating Bars

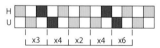

Warp: 3x2/16, dark green and mauve

Weft: 3x2/16, mauve

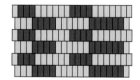

Uneven-length Overlapping Bars

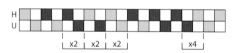

Warp: 3x2/16, dark green and mauve

Weft: 3x2/16, mauve

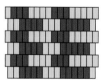

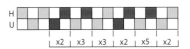

Separated Single Ends

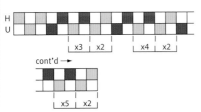

cont'd →

Warp: 3x2/16, dark green and mauve

Weft: 3x2/16, mauve

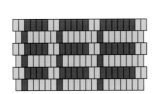

Separated Doubled Ends

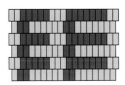

Warp: 3x2/16, dark green and mauve

Weft: 3x2/16, mauve

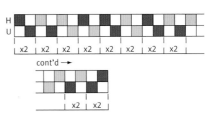

Single Ends, Interlinking and as Edging

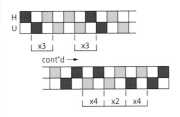

cont'd →

Warp: 3x2/16, dark green and mauve

Weft: 3x2/16, dark green

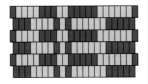

Doubled Ends, Interlinking and as Edging

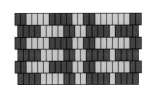

cont'd →

Warp: 3x2/16, dark green and mauve

Weft: 3x2/16, dark green

Tubular

The total number of warp threads must always be an odd number. The absolute minimum is 13, but 15 is a much more realistic number. Simple vertical patterns are best, as these provide a clearer image once the weaving is off the loom and twisted.

The weaving technique is slightly different: The shuttle always enters from the same side; then the weft is taken either over or under the inkle band, before it is reinserted from the same side for the next pick.

The sequence is:
1. Open next shed, beat, and tug.
2. Insert weft under tension and pull tight.
3. Roll tube with first finger and thumb.
4. Return weft to insertion side of band.

The direction of the weft insertion as well as the return path of the weft to the insertion edge determines the angle of twist: S or Z as the angle of the center of the capital letter.

The direction of insertion into the warp is marked with a horizontal arrow.

The return path of the weft is marked by a curve either above the arrow (to go over the inkle band) or below the arrow (to go under the inkle band).

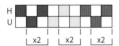

These tubes were all woven on the same warp.

3x2/16: dark green x5, cream x5, pink x5

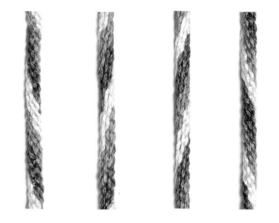

Insertion from right, return path over	Insertion from left, return path over	Insertion from right, return path under	Insertion from left, return path under
(__) ←	(__) →	← (__)	→ (__)
S-twist	Z-twist	Z-twist	S-twist

A change from right to left insertion can be made anywhere. To change the pathway from over to under, weave a short flat section in between.

Starting: No warp sticks; cross the weft and tail after the first pick, insert the tail from the opposite side.

Finishing: Insert loop protruding at insertion side.

When the inkle band is taken from the loom, the twist will not be dramatic. Overtwist in the natural direction and tug sharply. When released, the inkle will maintain a good twist.

Warning: It is very easy for the weft either to untwist and weaken or to over-twist and tangle during weaving. Check frequently so that the correct twist is maintained; otherwise, the weft may break. A slight over-twist is fine.

Tubular 1

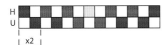

Warp: 3x2/16, dark green, cream, and pink

Weft: dark green

The reverse is inside the tube.

⟵ over S-twist

Taking the weft over the inkle band to reinsert it is the easiest method, as you can see the join more easily.

For a direct change to Z-twist:

⟶ over Z-twist

Change with 7 flat picks.

⟶ under S-twist

Tubular 2

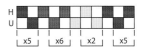

Warp: 3x2/16, dark green, cream, and pink

Weft: dark green

⟶ under S-twist

The tube is hollow and can be flattened if required.

Change with 13 flat picks.

⟵ over S-twist

This is worked around a core of 13 dark green 3x2/16 threads.

The maximum size of the core should be no more than ⅓ of the total size of all the grouped warp ends, although it can be less.

Weaving around a core is, of necessity, worked using the over-pathway method.

The warp may need to be eased round the core when working.

Tie the core to spare threads at the beginning of the warp, then hang the core over both top and joining pegs, using a medium weight on the end. Do not use a heddle around the core.

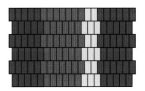

Repp Weave

Repp, rep, ripsmatta, matta, warp rib—these are all names for the same weave structure. As it is warp-faced and produces a thick, firm fabric, it is a natural technique for the inkle loom.

The loom is usually warped to make bars of alternating colors for heddled and unheddled threads, then thick and thin wefts are used in alternate picks, producing a marked horizontal rib effect. Where the thick wefts are used, one warp color will dominate on the face of the inkle band, and the alternate color will dominate on the reverse.

The thin weft is inserted into every pick to keep the edges firm. The thick weft is placed in every alternate pick. When you wish to make the other color dominant, you just place the thick weft into the opposite shed. The changeover can be made either by placing two thin wefts adjacent or two thick wefts adjacent.

There are several methods of working with the thick weft. It can be wound around a separate shuttle, left as a long length and inserted with the fingers, or halved and inserted from both sides at once. Successive colored thick wefts can be used in rotation. The thin weft could be finer than the warp threads, although they are the same in the samples here. The thick weft needs to be at least four times as thick as the thin weft. In the given samples, they are all twelve times as thick in the shed.

When working, it is best to take the thin weft under the thick weft at the edges. It is also best to insert the thin weft into the thick pick before inserting the thick weft, as this helps to hold the previous pick in place.

To weave the thick weft from alternate sides, either with a shuttle or a long length in the fingers:

Thin pick: Tug, insert thin weft, change shed, beat.

Thick pick: Open shed, beat, tug thin weft, insert thin weft, insert thick weft, change shed, and beat.

To weave the thick weft using two halves by crossover method: For the thick pick, insert the thin weft, then insert a half-size thick weft from both sides at once, holding them both at an upward angle. Pull to firm at the edges and draw both down to the fell. This way neither appears below the other one at the sides. Change shed and beat as usual.

When rotating the different-colored wefts, make sure to take the weft threads either over or under the other(s) in the same way—one could be always above, or they can alternate.

Because the thin weft is stabilizing the structure, the thick weft need not be pulled tightly to the edges—it can form decorative loops of various sizes as you wish.

One method of starting to use the thick weft is to halve it and insert it in the first pick. It can then be used from both sides, as in crossover, or from alternating sides by catching it around one thread at the edge of the inkle and carefully returning in the same shed so that the two halves are on the same side.

When you start weaving, the dominance of the warp color passing over the thick picks in the block will not be so very obvious until the alternate block is woven as a comparison.

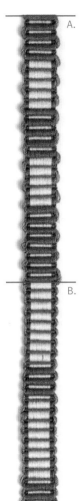

Repp 1

Single Insertion Method

Warp: 2/16, dark green and cream

Thin Weft: 2/16, dark green

Thick Weft: 4 strands dark green 3x2/16 wound onto one shuttle

A. Alternate thick weft with thin weft.

Crossover Method

Thin Weft: 2/16, dark green

Thick Wefts: 2 shuttles each wound with 2 strands 3x2/16, dark green

B. For thick weft, take both thick shuttles through the shed, starting them from opposite sides.

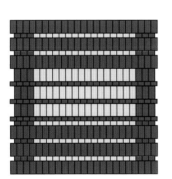

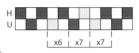

Repp 2

Warp: 2/16, dark green and cream

Thin Weft: 2/16, dark green

Thick Wefts: 2 shuttles with 2 strands 3x2/16, dark green; 2 shuttles with 2 strands 3x2/16, yellow

A. **Thick weft:** 1 dark green, 1 yellow started from opposite sides.

B. **Thick weft:** 2 shuttles green started from each side in 1st thick weft; 2 shuttles yellow started from each side in 2nd thick weft. Repeat.

C. **Thick weft:** 2 halved green and 2 halved yellow in alternate picks, with one color on top on both sides.

D. **Thick weft:** 2 each halved green and yellow, one color up on one side; the other on the other side.

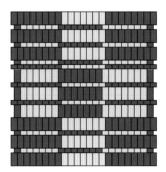

Designing Basic Warp Color Patterns

A warping draft gives no indication of what the finished inkle pattern will look like, so you need to be able to create a representation of the finished inkle.

As already noted (see page 6), the basic structure of an inkle is warp-faced tabby, with the upper and lower layers of the warp threads crowding together and the individual threads of one warp layer indented from those of the next.

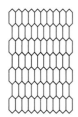

True structure of an inkle

Trying to design on this ovoid grid, however, is not easy; but by simplifying the grid—making the ovals into rectangles—it becomes easier to see the sequential layers, while the indentation is retained. Each rectangle equals one warp thread as it shows on the surface. The 2:1 height-to-width ratio reflects the length of the pick in relation to the width of the warp thread. A tabby pattern repeats pick-and-pick, so to see the sequence of a design properly, a minimum of six picks is needed.

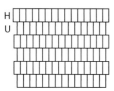

Draw a line under the two top lines and mark these H (heddled) and U (unheddled) at the sides. Even though the pattern actually develops upward on the loom, it is often easier to design from the top downward.

Whatever colors are inserted into the H line must be repeated exactly in alternate rows; colors inserted into the U line are likewise repeated.

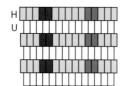 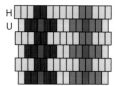

Coloring in all the H rows first and then the U rows in between helps to position the colors in the U rows to create specific patterns.

TIP:

Lightly shade in the main pattern sequence in pencil (just one color on white) before coloring the rectangles in with your preferred color. That way you can correct it easily if you don't like the ensuing design.

The samples provided show several basic ideas for patterns and color combinations. By combining several different patterns and colors in your own configurations, you can create your own unique patterns.

Choosing the required width of the design chart

First, determine how many warp threads you will need for the width you require (see page 6). You will need a pattern chart with half that total number of warp threads along the H row. (With an odd number of warp threads, the H row will contain one more warp thread than the U row.)

Pattern charts can be found on pages 167–170.

If the pattern chart is too wide, draw a line at the right-hand side to suit.

Note how this zigzags down the graph.

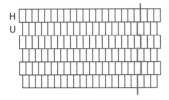

If the pattern chart is too narrow, cut a second chart to dovetail with the first.

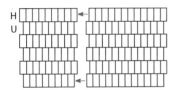

Rather than coloring a wide section of the chart, a single color border can just be indicated at the edges.

Remember to consider the color of the weft. If you want the weft to merge with the color of the selvedges, the edges of the design must both be the same color as the weft.

Making a warping draft

To transfer the pattern chart to a warping draft, fill in every alternate square on the H row of the draft with the sequence of colors along the H row of the pattern chart and the intermediate squares on the U row of the draft with the colors on the U row of the pattern chart.

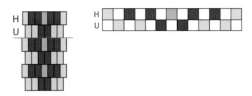

Or you could just write in the initial letter of the colors.

H	Y		B		B		G		B		B		Y
U		Y		Y		B		B		Y		Y	

You could also read the warping sequence from the pattern chart, alternating between the H row and the U row.

Warp Manipulation

Pick-up

Warp manipulation covers an extremely wide range of different techniques in which selected warp threads are moved from their normal position to the opposite layer for one pick. These warp threads can either be lifted up from the lower layer to the upper or pushed down from the upper layer to the lower. Both the actual warping draft and the way the threads are moved contribute to the individual techniques. Several of the different techniques have acquired the word *pick-up* as a suffix—a misnomer when push down is part of the process.

I prefer to use the name pick-up *only* for the variety of techniques where warp threads are lifted, or picked up, from the lower layer to the upper. Other warp-manipulated techniques are given their own specific title.

In pick-up, the lower layer can be heddled or un-heddled. A pick-up can be made by always picking unheddled warp threads up into the heddled layer, by always picking up heddled warp threads to join the unheddled layer, or by a combination of the two. When either heddled or unheddled threads are picked up, the pick-up is made on alternate picks. When a combination pick-up is used, the pick-up needs to be made on every pick. The shed where the pick-up takes place is referred to as the pick-up shed. Usually the pick-up covers a horizontally striped background, which is formed naturally. When using a combined pick-up, this background can be virtually covered. Note page 39, which shows all three patterns: H, U, and striped.

Usually alternate warp threads are picked up. As each picked-up thread passes over three picks (the natural pick, the picked-up pick, and the natural pick again), the yarn is able to relax and dominate the threads under them. Sometimes two adjacent (pairs of) threads are picked up from the lower layer; however, this means that the weft is floating over five warp threads on the underside of the inkle, so it isn't a good idea to pick up more than two adjacent warp threads. (Occasionally, a picked-up warp thread will float over five picks including the start and finish row.)

The easiest method is to pick up unheddled threads, as these are more movable. First, open the shed with the unheddled threads in the upper layer; beat, tug, and weave. Change the shed so that the heddled warp threads are in the top layer; beat, and then pick up those unheddled warp threads from the lower layer that are required to join the upper layer; beat again to confirm, tug, and weave. Change the shed, beat, tug, and weave.

Reading the pattern charts

This pattern chart shows ONLY the unheddled threads as filled rectangles.

Where the unheddled threads are naturally in the lower layer they are shaded in gray, while the picked-up warp threads are colored in their respective colors, passing over the heddled layer (white row). The heddled threads are in the blank (white) row in between the unheddled (shaded) row.

Always read pick-up charts from the bottom row up, in the direction in which you weave.

To differentiate between picking up unheddled and heddled warp threads, the heddled warp threads to be picked up are shown as colored lines between the colored or shaded rectangles.

Here the sequence starts with the heddled threads in the upper layer; weave as usual.

Change to the unheddled shed, pick up and add the heddled threads required for that shed and beat, tug, and weave.

Change to the heddled shed, beat, tug, and weave.

The picked-up heddled threads pass over the shaded unheddled layer. The beginning and end of each picked-up heddled thread is marked with a short bar.

It is necessary to have a charting method to distinguish the heddled and unheddled threads when both are combined in a single pattern. Unheddled picked-up threads are shown as solid rectangles; heddled picked-up threads are shown as narrow lines between the shaded rectangles, with the starting and finishing points as a short bar. (These can be thought of as the heddles.)

To manipulate the pick-up

The warp threads to be picked up can be selected separately or with the pick-up shed open. Once the pattern is established, it is easy to see where threads need to be picked up because of the previous pattern.

Separately

Beat the pick-up shed open, then, without weaving, reopen the previous shed and place the threads to be picked up on a short, thin, flat stick. Push this to the fell, open the pick-up shed again and add the picked-up warp threads on the stick to those that are naturally in the upper layer; beat again, tug, and insert weft to weave.

With the pick-up shed open

Beat open, insert first two fingers of both hands into the shed, then separate those threads in the upper layer at the various points where you need to pick up threads from the lower layer. Pick up all the threads needed manually and add them to the upper-layer threads already held; beat again, tug, and insert weft to weave.

Reverses

Reverse sides are shown, even when there is very little to see on the reverse.

Singles, Unheddled

Warp: 3x2/16 navy and pale green

Weft: 3x2/16 pale green

Single Unheddled 1

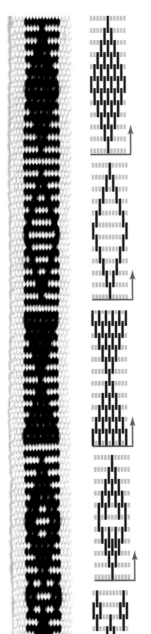

Single Unheddled 2

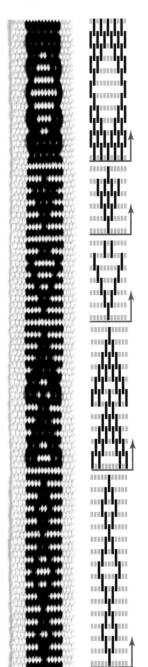

Warp: 3x2/16, navy and pale green

Weft: 3x2/16, pale green

The reverse sides do not show clearly, because the picked-up threads are replaced by the same color weft thread.

Single Heddled 1

Single Heddled 2

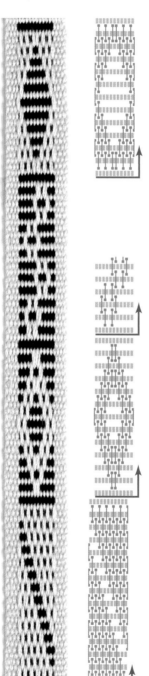

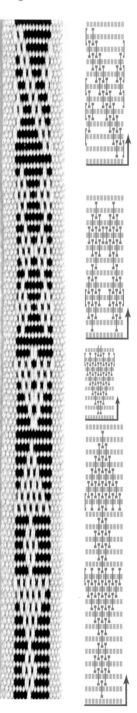

Pairs, Unheddled

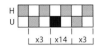

H
U

x3 | x14 | x3

Pair Unheddled 1

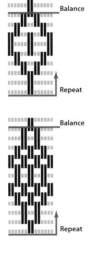

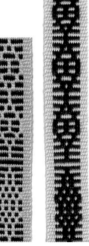

Balance
Repeat

Balance
Repeat

Balance
Repeat

Balance
Repeat

Balance
Repeat

Balance
Repeat

Pair Unheddled 2

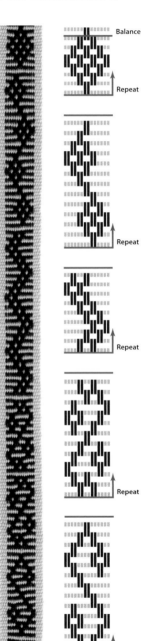

Balance
Repeat

Repeat

Repeat

Repeat

Repeat

Combined Singles and Pairs, Unheddled

Warp: 2/16 navy and lime green

Weft: 2/16 lime green

Singles and Pairs 1

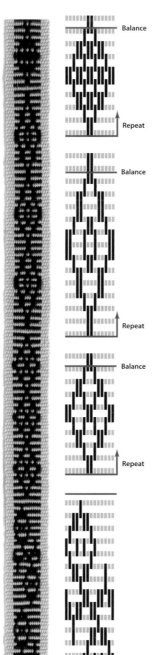

Balance

Repeat

Balance

Repeat

Balance

Repeat

Singles and Pairs 2

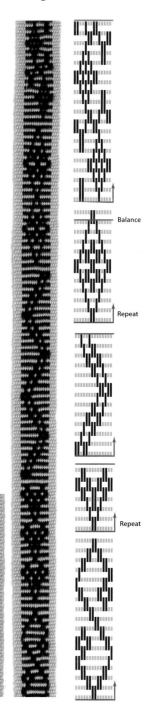

Balance

Repeat

Repeat

Repeat

Combined, Unheddled and Heddled

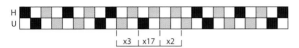

H
U

x3 x17 x2

Warp: 2/16, navy and pale blue
Weft: 2/16, navy

Mixed 1

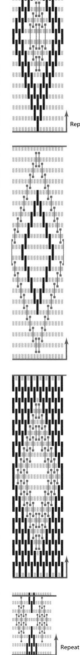

Repeat

Repeat

Repeat

Mixed 2

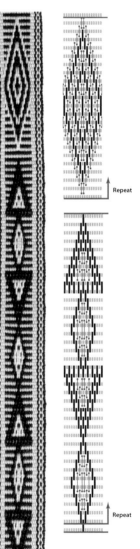

Repeat

Repeat

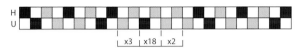

H
U

x3 | x18 | x2

Mixed 4

Note number of repeats for bar.

Warp: 2/16, navy and pale blue

Weft: 2/16, navy

Mixed 4

Decrease and increase the shapes along the diagonal lines.

Only the changes in pick-up are charted.

Weave the sample beginning with the pattern at the bottom.

Mixed 3

Balance

Repeat

Repeat

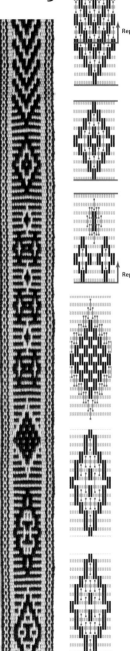

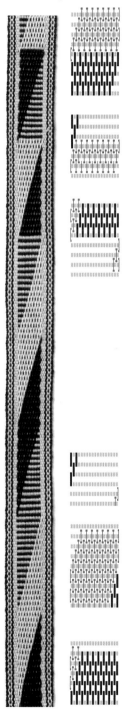

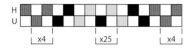

x4   x25   x4

Warp: 2/16, navy, cream, and orange

Weft: 2/16, orange

Single Unheddled 1

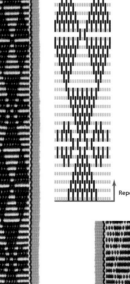

Repeat

Derived from a Guatemalan design.

Repeat

Single Unheddled 2

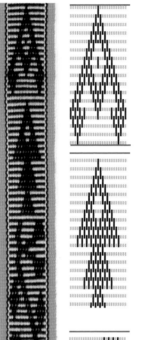

"Hands on Hips"—derived from a Turkish carpet design that means "made by a woman"!

A fish—a common design in many cultures.

Trailing vine.

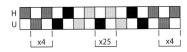

Warp: 2/16, navy, cream, and orange

Weft: 2/16, orange

Singles and Pairs 1

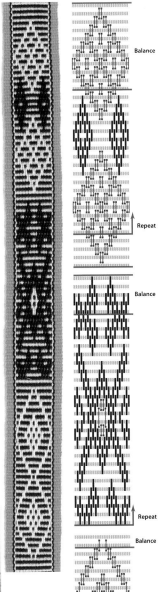

Singles and Pairs 2

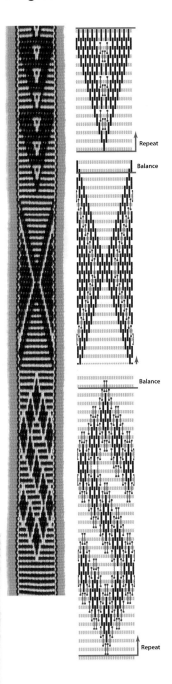

Combined, Unheddled and Heddled

Mixed 1

Warp: 3x2/16, navy and yellow
Weft: 3x2/16, yellow

Mixed 2

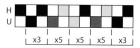

Warp: 3x2/16 navy, red, and yellow
Weft: 3x2/16, navy

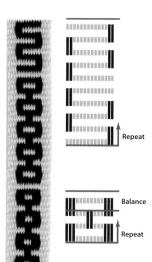

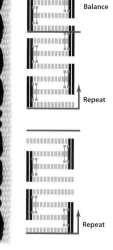

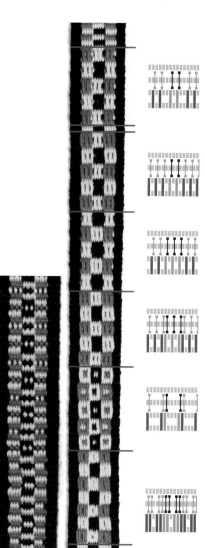

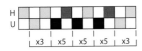

Warp: 3x2/16 navy, red, and yellow

Weft: 3x2/16 navy, red, and yellow

Colors and Floats 1

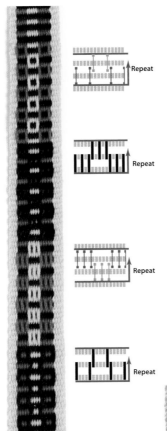

Colors and Floats 2

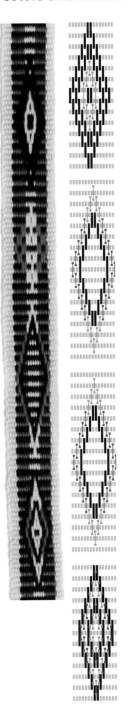

Designing pick-up

Use the chart on page 167, which is like this:

The grid lines have been removed so that heddled and unheddled pick-ups can be inserted.

The shaded rectangles are the unheddled warp pattern threads; the blank rows are the heddled warp threads.

Unheddled pick-ups are colored and shaded rectangles, including the shaded rectangles at the start and finish, and pass over unshaded rows. Floats may extend over three or five rows, but no more. If a longer length is required, split it into two shorter lengths, such as a length of seven split into two floats of three with a tie-down (one non-float) in between.

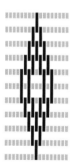

Normally, alternate warp threads are picked up to prevent overlong floats on the reverse. However, pairs are occasionally used in a combined pick-up, to balance at the center of a motif and as a specific technique.

Mark your design on the chart lightly in pencil so that you can erase mistakes; color it in after the design is complete.

The shaded row will always be the color of the unheddled threads, and the blank rows indicate the heddled threads. These are usually left uncolored on the design chart because it easier to read the chart if only the threads that are actually being manipulated are highlighted by color.

Heddled threads are shown as starting and finishing the pick-up on a blank row, with the threads passing between the shaded rectangles as they float.

Lettering: Compensating Method

There are several methods of working letters on the inkle loom. I devised this method to fit the following criteria: as few warp threads as possible were to be displaced from their correct (natural) position, the surface floats were to be as short as possible, the height of the letter was to be greater than the width, the crossbars were to be as thick as the upright strokes, and the back of the inkle was to be as neat as the front.

Many letters have, or can have, a complete upright stroke: B, D, E, F, H, I, K, L, M, N, P, R, T, and W, while others can be added to this list if the rounded letters are squared at the corners: C, G, J, O, Q, U, and Y. A can also be squared at the top, but three of the remaining letters: V, X, and Z must keep their diagonal lines to remain distinguishable. The remaining letter S has a small bite out of the two uprights with three crossbars.

With the preponderance of uprights, it seemed sensible to create the letters on a basic bar threading. The threads used for lettering are heddled to make it easier to work the unheddled threads as an alternating single pick-up in between words.

It is usually easier to see the woven letters clearly if the lettering threads are dark and the background light. The light background also extends to surround the dark lettering bar.

Reading drafts for lettering

A warping draft for compensating lettering would be similar to this:

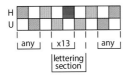

The lettering threads are red and the background cream in this example.

There are thirteen lettering threads.

Any pattern can be placed in the borders or elsewhere in the warping draft, but there needs to be a minimum of eight warp ends total on either side of the lettering section to help to stabilize the inkle.

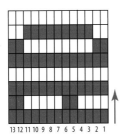

When weaving, the letters and numerals are worked sideways, in the normal direction they are written, the bars used for the uprights. Although the letters and numerals look very angular on the charts, they are more rounded when woven.

NOTE:

The lettering charts show only where the dark lettering threads must be in the upper layer of the shed. The white rectangles are not the background threads—rather, they are the lettering threads that must lie in the lower layer of the shed.

Within a single pick it is often necessary to manipulate both dark and/or light threads into an upper or lower shed to create the correct shape for the letter or numeral. To avoid a gap where threads have been repositioned, threads of the opposite color need to take their place—exchanging their positions.

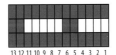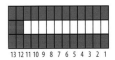

Obviously, elements of the letters that are formed with a complete upright do not require any manipulation at all.

NOTE:

In a dark shed or dark pick, the dark lettering threads are on the top layer; a light shed is when the light background threads are on the top layer. Lettering threads within the bands are numbered from right to left (13, 12, 11, ... 3, 2, 1).

Letters are formed over an odd number of picks (either one, three, or five).

After the completion of each letter, weave one light pick to separate it from the next letter.

Because so many letters are composed of uprights, the instructions start by showing how to lift the dark lettering threads to the upper layer of a normally light shed. Use two short double-pointed knitting needles or shed sticks to pick up the threads.

1. Open the light shed and beat.

2. Push the light threads down and pick up the required dark threads with the first needle; push this to the fell (toward the last pick woven) of the inkle:

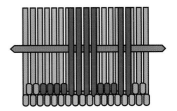

3. Lift all the light threads above the dark in the usual way:

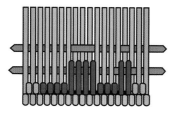

Using the second needle, select all the border threads and all the light threads except those that are within the outer edges of the blocks of dark threads that have already been selected. This effectively depresses or puts down the light threads in the areas where the dark threads have been selected.

Join the two sets of selected threads together and weave that pick.

Per block there will be one fewer light thread put down than there are dark threads picked up.

EXAMPLE: How to weave U

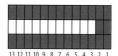

1. Weave a complete dark pick. (This is the first upright of the letter U.)

2. Change the shed and beat.

3. Push the light threads down and pick up dark lettering threads 1 and 2 on the first needle. Push the needle to the fell of the inkle.

4. Lift the light shed and insert the second needle into it, skipping over the one light thread that lies between the two dark lifted threads on the first needle. Remember that all border threads need to be on this needle as well.

5. Join the two sets of threads on the needles and weave the pick.

6. Change the shed and beat. Weave this dark pick for the last upright of the letter U.

7. Change the shed, beat, and weave the light pick to finish the letter.

EXAMPLE: How to weave A

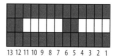

1. Weave a complete dark pick. (This is the first upright of the letter A.)

2. Change the shed and beat.

3. Push the light threads down and pick up dark lettering threads 5 and 6 and 12 and 13 on the first needle. Push the needle to the fell of the inkle.

4. Lift the light shed and insert the second needle into it, skipping over the two single light threads that lie between each of the pairs of dark lifted threads on the first needle. Remember that all the bordering threads must be on the needle as well.

5. Join the two sets of threads on the needles and weave the pick.

6. Change the shed and beat. Weave this dark pick, the last upright of the letter A.

7. Change the shed, beat, and weave the light pick to finish the letter.

Light thread, dark shed

The following instructions are for when light threads are to be brought to the surface of a normally dark shed.

1. Open the dark shed and beat:

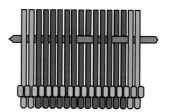

2. With the first needle, select all border threads PLUS the required dark threads, then push the needle to the fell of the inkle:

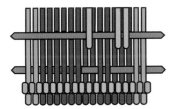

3. Working with one block at a time, lift the light threads that lie between each block of lifted dark threads. Do not pick up the two light threads that are on either side of the dark threads. Place the selected light threads on the second needle as you work.

Again, there will be one fewer light thread than discarded dark threads.

Join the two sets of selected threads together and weave that pick.

EXAMPLE: How to weave C

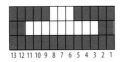

1. Weave a complete dark pick for the first upright of the letter C.

2. Change the shed and beat.

3. Push the light threads down and pick up dark lettering threads 1 and 2 and 12 and 13 on the first needle. Push the needle to the fell of the inkle.

4. Lift the light shed and insert the second needle into it, skipping over the two single light threads that lie between the two pairs of lifted dark threads on the first needle. Remember that all border threads must be on the needle as well.

5. Join the two sets of threads on the needles and weave the pick.

6. Change the shed and beat. (This is a dark shed.)

7. Place all the threads onto the second needle, except for the dark lettering threads 6, 7, and 8. Push the needle to the fell of the inkle.

8. Lift and place on the second needle the two threads that lie in between the three skipped-over dark threads.

9. Join the two sets of threads and weave the pick.

10. Change the shed, beat, and weave the light pick to finish the letter.

EXAMPLE: How to weave M, a five-pick letter.

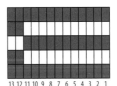

1. Weave a complete dark pick for the first upright of the letter M.

2. Change the shed and beat.

3. Push the light threads down and pick up the dark lettering threads 12 and 13 on the first needle. Push the needle to the fell of the inkle.

4. Lift the light shed and insert the second needle, skipping over the one light thread lying between the two lifted dark threads on the first needle. Remember that all border threads must be on this needle as well.

5. Join the two sets of threads on the needles and weave the pick.

6. Change the shed and beat. (This is a dark shed.)

7. Place all the threads onto the first needle, except for lettering threads 12 and 13.

8. Lift and place on the second needle the one light thread that lies between the two discarded dark threads.

9. Join the two sets of threads and weave the pick.

10. Change the shed and beat.

11. Push the light threads down and pick up dark lettering threads 12 and 13 on the first needle. Push the needle to the fell of the inkle.

12. Lift the light shed and insert the second needle into it, skipping over the one light thread lying between the two lifted dark threads on the first needle. All border threads must be on this needle as well.

13. Join the two sets of threads on the needles and weave the pick.

14. Change the shed and beat. Weave the pick to form the final upright of the letter M.

15. Change the shed, beat, and weave the light pick to finish the letter.

When weaving letters or numerals that do not have a complete upright at the start or finish, only beat gently when changing to the next pick or the letter may become distorted.

This is especially true when weaving T, L, P, E, or F.

EXAMPLE: How to weave T. (This is a five-pick letter so that the upright appears in the correct pick.)

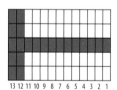

13 12 11 10 9 8 7 6 5 4 3 2 1

1. Open the dark shed. Place the dark lettering threads 12 and 13 onto the first needle as well as all the border threads.

2. Lift all the light threads that lie in between the depressed dark lettering threads. Place these on the second needle.

3. Join the two sets of threads on the needles and weave the pick.

4. Change the shed to the light shed and beat.

5. Lift the dark shed. Pick up dark threads 12 and 13 onto the first needle.

6. Lift the light shed and insert the second needle into it, discarding the one light thread that lies between the two dark lifted threads on the first needle. (Remember that all border threads must be on this needle as well.)

7. Join the two sets of threads on the needles and weave the pick.

8. Change the shed and beat gently to form a dark shed and the center upright of the letter T. Weave this pick.

9. Change to the light shed and beat gently.

10. Lift the dark shed. Pick up dark threads 12 and 13 onto the first needle.

11. Lift the light shed and insert the second needle, skipping over the one light thread between the two lifted dark threads on the first needle. Remember that all border threads must be on this needle as well.

12. Join the two sets of threads on the needles and weave the pick.

13. Change the shed to a dark shed and beat.

14. Place all the border threads plus the dark lettering threads 12 and 13 onto the first needle. Lift all light threads that lie in between dark lettering threads and place them on the second needle.

15. Join the two sets of threads and weave this pick.

16. Change the shed; beat this light pick gently. Weave to finish the letter.

Weave five picks between words: three light and two dark. Pick up alternating light threads on the first dark pick and the opposite light threads on the second dark pick.

See page 52 for more information.

Reverses

These are not shown because they have no significance.

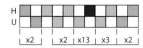

Warp: 3x2/16, brown, cream, and turquoise

Weft: 3x2/16, turquoise

3-Pick Letters 1

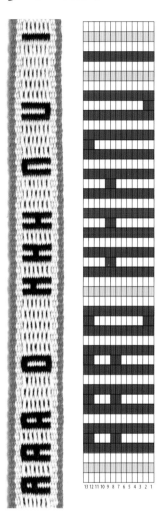

These letters all start and end with a complete upright.

The only single-pick letter is I.

Letters with one bar: H, N, U.

Letters with two bars: A, O.

3-Pick Letters 2

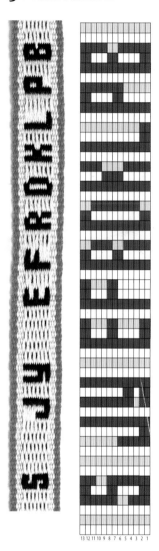

These letters are open-sided.

Open-sided exit: E, F, R, D, K, L, P, B.

Open-sided entry: J, Y.

Open-sided entry and exit: S.

Letters and Numerals

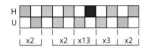

H
U

| x2 | | x2 | x13 | x3 | x2 |

Letters:

Warp: 3x2/16, brown, cream, and turquoise

Weft: 3x2/16, turquoise

Numerals:

Warp: 2/16, brown, cream, and turquoise

Weft: 2/16, turquoise

5-Pick Letters

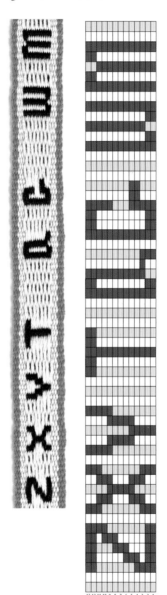

W, M

T, Q, G

Z, X, Y

Numerals

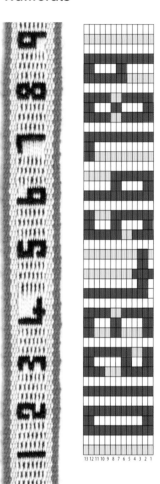

7, 8, 9

4, 5, 6

0, 1, 2, 3

Between words

A single light pick separates individual letters, but a longer space is needed between words. Use 5 picks total:

1. The last light pick at the end of the letter.

2. A dark pick with every other light thread picked up and no dark threads put down.

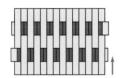

3. A light pick.

4. A second dark pick with the opposite alternate threads picked up—again, no dark threads put down.

5. A third light pick.

Make this 5-pick separation section before and after each word. It may be extended to more picks to extend the space between words.

Patterns may also be added before and after the pick-up separation section.

Because there are 13 dark lettering threads with 14 light threads surrounding them, the number of alternately picked-up light threads on each of the dark picks will be 7, and they will be offset from one another:

In the instructions that follow, the light threads that are picked up to the right of the lettering bar are the Right Pick-up threads (RP):

and those that complete the sequence just after (to the left of) the dark lettering bar are the Left Pick-up threads (LP):

Letters with an incomplete upright at either the beginning or end sometimes need special consideration as to which of the two alternative pick-up sequences to use between letters.

When entering or exiting a letter, sometimes an LP or a RP may be the best pick-up to use. If the letter has an incomplete upright at the beginning or the end, then it is preferable to choose the pick-up next to it so that there are the minimum floats of light threads continuing into the letter. However, this is not always possible, especially when two letters vie for best sequence. In these cases, a choice has to be made between the two.

Between the words

Use the chart at right to determine the best pick-up sequence (LP or RP) to use before starting or after completing a letter.

(RP is marked R and LP is marked L.)

If there is no check in the row, either of the sequences is suitable.

Double check marks are more imperative than single checks.

Sometimes it is impossible to choose, such as when L or T occurs at the end of one word and is followed by T or Z at the beginning of the next. A similar dilemma occurs when E or S is followed by S or J at the beginning of the next word.

Choose the pick-up sequence that is least likely to obtrude.

When letters have a single light float in the upright, avoid having a float extend from the picked-up separation section.

	into	out of
A		
B		R ✓✓
C		
D		
E		R ✓✓
F		L ✓
G		L ✓✓
H		
I		
J	R ✓✓	
K		L ✓✓
L		R ✓✓
M		
N		
O		
P		L ✓✓
Q		L ✓✓
R		L ✓✓
S	R ✓✓	R ✓✓
T	L ✓	L ✓
U		
V		
W		
X		
Y	R ✓✓	
Z	L ✓✓	R ✓✓
1		
2	R ✓✓	
3	R ✓✓	R ✓✓
4	R ✓	R ✓✓
5	R ✓✓	
6		
7	L ✓	
8	R ✓✓	R ✓✓
9	R ✓	
0		
?	R ✓✓	R ✓✓
!	R ✓✓	R ✓✓

Runic

This technique was the result of a happy experiment when I decided to allow distortions when weaving with the compensating lettering technique. Why runic? Because the resulting patterns reminded me of the incised runic script on Scandinavian stone monuments.

It works better with a longer contrast bar than the one used for the lettering because the additional width gives a greater opportunity for the angle of the weft to distort.

Only a few border threads on either side should be used—about six in total. Otherwise it is difficult to distort the angle of the weft.

The number of threads in the contrast bar needs to be about twenty-six to thirty.

The technique is to beat firmly at all times, including rocking the shuttle (beater) from side to side across the shed to emphasize the curving angle of weft distortion.

The sequence is:

1. Heddled threads up, beat hard, tug.

    Pick up the heddled threads required both from the pattern and all those in the borders and place them on the first needle, push to fell.

    Lift the unheddled threads that lie in the gaps left by the heddled pattern threads that were not picked up onto the first needle and place these selected threads on the second needle.

    There will be one fewer picked-up thread than discarded heddled threads.

    Join the two sets of selected threads and weave that pick. (See instructions for Lettering: Compensating Method, page 44.)

2. Unheddled threads up, beat hard, tug.

    Push the unheddled threads down and pick up the heddled threads that are required with the first needle; push this to the fell of the inkle.

Lift all the unheddled threads up and using the second needle, select all the border threads and all the unheddled threads except those that are within the outer edges of the heddled threads already selected.

(This effectively puts down those unheddled threads in the areas where the heddled threads have been selected.) There will be one fewer unheddled thread put down than heddled threads picked up.

Join the two sets of selected threads and weave that pick.

Warp draft as above.

Warp and weft: 3x2/16

Reverse

By creating an imbalance in areas of alternately woven picks and floats, the weft is forced to curve, then by repeating the imbalance at the other side, the angle of the curve is altered.

The reverse shows shapes similar to the front but with unheddled threads forming the shapes.

No specific instructions are given, apart from the first sample, as there is no specific sequence of repeat patterning.

The contrast bar could also be placed on the unheddled threads, but as both sets of threads are manipulated throughout, and the compensating technique has already been described, the instructions are for the contrast bar to be on heddled threads.

Runic

Runic 1

Warp: 2/16, border: pale blue, multicolor where shown as orange; bar: brown

Weft: 2/16, pale blue

A. Alternate single Y shapes with the fork to right and then left (inverse);

   Length of upright (float) is always 16 pick-ups.

B. Alternate 2XY with doubled forks to right and left; random length pick-ups.

C. Sunrise, Sunset completely random Y-shapes and pick-ups. Look at reverse for reason for title.

Runic 2

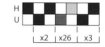

Warp: 2/16, border: brown, striped red, and orange where shown as red; bar: cream

Weft: 2/16, brown

A. Alternating 3xY and inverse; random length pick-ups.

B. Y shape plus extra short lengths; random length pick-ups.

C. Includes center short lengths and gaps; random length pick-ups.

Lettering on Checks

Traditionally, letters made on checked patterns are produced by five groups of two different blocks, each block consisting of three lettering-colored warps alternated with three background-colored warp threads. In the second block, the two colors exchange heddled or unheddled positions. When woven without manipulation, this threading creates a false check, and two threads the same color appear at the intersections of blocks. If a true check is threaded, however, so that each block consists of three lettering-colored threads with two background threads lying between them, and these blocks are warped alternately (one with the lettering colors heddled, the next with the lettering colors unheddled), no adjacent nonlettering threads will occur.

The advantage of this method is that diagonal lines can be made in letters that require them; the disadvantages are that no complete uprights are available in this method, and every pick has to be manipulated.

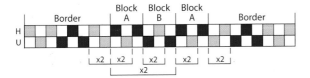

5-Block checks

I have adapted the technique, using blocks of true checks, to create the letters and numerals.

When woven without warp manipulation, the 5-group weaving draft will look like this:

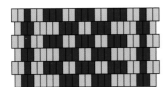

Any border patterns can be added, but the background color should be used to warp the selvedge and for the weft.

Although the pattern areas of the warping drafts here start with Block A, it doesn't matter whether

they begin with an A block (three heddled lettering threads) or a B block (three unheddled lettering threads). It doesn't matter which pick is selected to start any letter; it doesn't matter which pick finishes the letter. All threads within the blocks can be manipulated up or down.

When it is necessary to pick up the lettering threads, all three in the block are lifted and both background threads are put down. For background colors on the surface, all the lettering threads in the block are put down, and both the background colors are picked up.

Use a weft the same color as the background warp threads. When the background threads are on the surface, there will be one fewer per block than there are lettering threads. This means that the weft can show very slightly between the warp threads when the background is woven. When the lettering threads are on the surface, they will cover the surface easily because there are more of them.

Between letters you make one background pick. Between words you can create an automatic small motif using the check patterning, with one or two picks between. Larger or more elaborate patterns can be used between sentences.

Possible patterns on 5-block checks

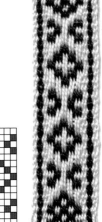

Weaving

When selecting the warp threads for a pick, first beat the previous pick. Then, working from either right to left or left to right (your preference), manipulate each block as required. This is easy to do just using fingers—use both hands in the shed.

Picking up lettering threads in a block: pick up a lettering thread, put down a background, pick up a lettering thread, put down a background, pick up the third lettering thread.

Picking up background threads in a block: put down a lettering thread, pick up a background, put down a lettering thread, pick up a background, put down the third lettering thread.

Beat the newly manipulated shed, tug, and weave. Change, beat, tug.

If you prefer to use a pick-up stick, work the stick through the shed in the same way: turn the stick on edge, place the weft through, remove the pick-up stick, change the shed, beat, tug.

There will inevitably be floats, some longer than others, grouped together. Always make sure that the weft in the previous pick is lying very straight after beating the new shed.

Letters are shown on squared paper five squares wide (the width of the letter). Each square represents one block of warp threads and each row one pick. Read the weaving chart from the bottom upward.

The samples are arranged in groups of the possible number of picks required to make the letter.

One pick: I

Three picks: A, B, C, D, E, F, H, J, L, N, O, P, S, T, U, Y

Four picks: B, D, E, F, G, J, K, L, O, Q, R, S, U, Y, Z

Five picks: all the letters except I

Several letters can be woven in two different ways, some in three. You may choose whichever style you prefer and even change styles from one letter to the next because the blocks are interchangeable when weaving.

7-block checks

From 5-block checks I devised this method for 7-block checks. The technique is the same, but all the letters are made over 5 picks (except for I), and all the numerals over 3 picks, except 4, which is made over 5 picks.

The advantage of the 7-block method is that all the letters and numerals are over an odd number of picks, which makes positioning matching patterns between words easier. The letters are also better proportioned. The disadvantage is that the 10 extra threads in the warp mean slightly more manipulation when weaving.

Reverses

Reverses are not shown, as lettering techniques are one-sided.

Possible patterns on 7-block checks

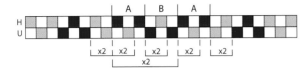

Warp: 2/16, brown and pale green

Weft: 2/16, pale green

Letters over 1, 3, and 4 Picks

Letters over 5 Picks

Numerals and Sentences on 5-Block Checks

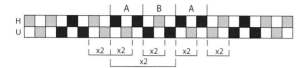

Warp: 2/16, brown and pale green

Weft: 2/16, pale green

Numbers and Patterns

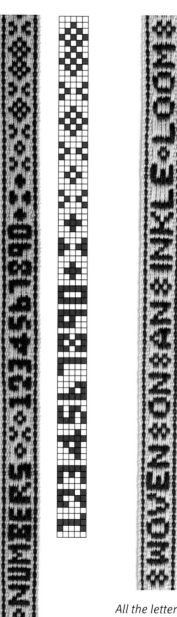

All the letters are made over 5 picks, with words separated by short patterns.

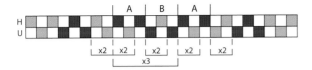

Warp: 2/16, brown and pale blue

Weft: 2/16, pale blue

Letters over 5 Picks (Except I)

Numerals over 3 Picks (except 4)

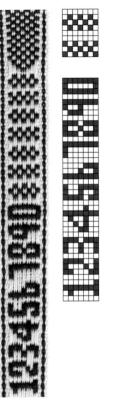

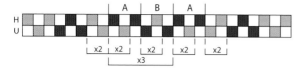

Warp: 2/16, brown and pale blue

Weft: 2/16, pale blue

7-Block Checks 1   7-Block Checks 2

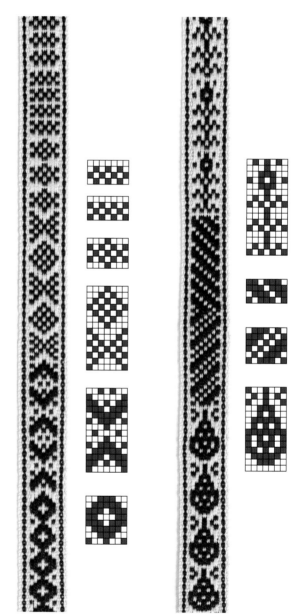

Baltic-Style Patterns

Narrow bands woven in this patterning technique are found extensively in the northern European countries around the Baltic Sea. The patterns are created with thicker (or doubled) warp pattern threads, manipulated as required, above the surface of a (usually) contrasting color background. These pattern threads can be manipulated both above and below the inkle and form patterns on both sides. Although the patterns all use the same technique there are regional and national variations in the designs and colors used.

Baltic-style woven bands are often used in the national costumes of the countries as horizontal bands around skirts and sleeves, vertical bands on waistcoats, and as suspenders for trousers, as well as for decoration on other items, and for tying and securing items. They were an essential part of life, from hanging the cradle to lowering the coffin into the grave; young girls wove them for their dowry chest.

Warping

The pattern areas for Baltic-style inkles are always warped in the same way: in repeats of 6 threads (a thick pattern thread, 2 finer background threads, a thick pattern thread, 2 finer background) all warped alternately as heddled and unheddled, plus a final pattern warp thread to balance, so that symmetrical as well as asymmetrical patterns can be woven.

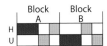

One unit of Baltic pattern warping draft

A great many patterns can be woven with as few as 5 pattern threads, and with more, the possibilities become almost endless.

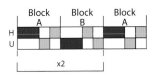

5-pattern threads in warping draft. The repeat numbers are altered for different numbers of pattern sizes.

The background threads within the pattern area are all the same color, originally usually of linen, with the pattern thread in wool. A border of the same type as the background threads is added on each side of the pattern area.

For the pattern threads in the following samples, either a thicker single thread or a double thread of the same thickness as the background is used. I have used cotton throughout.

Because the background weaves as a basketweave, it is best if the weft is of the same type and color as the background threads. Small specks of weft can show and could detract from the pattern if the colors contrast too much.

Weaving the background

Alternately raising and lowering the unheddled threads will result in small spots of the pattern threads, indented alternately in every pick, appearing both above and below the inkle.

Reading the pattern charts

Because Baltic-style pattern threads are thicker and they force the background threads apart, the pattern chart can be drawn on squared paper. Only the pattern threads are shown on the chart, with blank squares representing pattern threads that are in the lower layer of the inkle. Background threads are not shown in the chart, as they are not manipulated and will be raised and lowered naturally in normal weaving.

Pattern threads that appear in the top layer of the shed are indicated with alternating dots on the pattern chart. The red arrow shows the direction in which the pattern chart is read—upward—as that is the way your inkle will grow.

If a dotted square is colored, then that pattern thread is left above the inkle; if a dotted square is uncolored, then that pattern thread must be dropped down on that pick.

If an undotted square is colored, then that pattern thread has to be picked up on that pick.

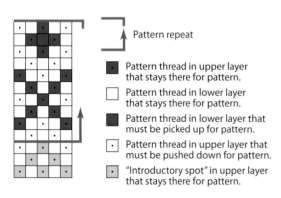

Pattern repeat

■ Pattern thread in upper layer that stays there for pattern.

☐ Pattern thread in lower layer that stays there for pattern.

■ Pattern thread in lower layer that must be picked up for pattern.

· Pattern thread in upper layer that must be pushed down for pattern.

· "Introductory spot" in upper layer that stays there for pattern.

The red horizontal line below the pattern repeat and adjoining the arrow shows the start of the pattern repeat.

The red horizontal line at the top of the pattern indicates the return to the start.

In addition to the pattern repeat areas, Baltic-style charts show lighter-colored introductory spots below the start line. These are a suggested way to organize the spots before starting the pattern and are not meant to be included in the pattern repeat.

To weave the patterns

Open the first shed, insert the index and second fingers of both hands, dropping down those pattern threads that are not required, and picking up any that are required from below.

Hold the new shed on one hand, insert the shuttle, beat, tug, and weave.

It is simple to pick up and drop down pattern threads entirely with the fingers because there are so few pattern threads, and it is rarely necessary to manipulate even half of them in any one pick.

Except for a row of basic dotted natural picks, some pattern threads will need to be manipulated in every pick.

Some rows require all the pattern threads to be dropped down: check carefully for these empty rows.

Reverses

The reverse sides of the Baltic-style inkles are shown, as the appearance of the patterns on the underside is so very interesting. Except for lettered patterns, there is no wrong side.

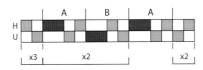

Warp: 3x2/16, pink and indigo
Weft: 3x2/16, pink

Baltic-5 1

Baltic-5 2

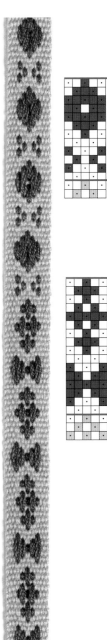

Baltic-Style 5

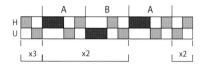

Warp: 3x2/16, pink and indigo
Weft: 3x2/16, pink

Baltic-5 3

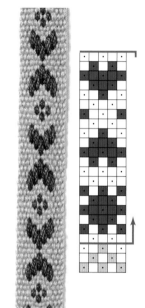

Baltic-5 4

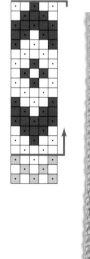

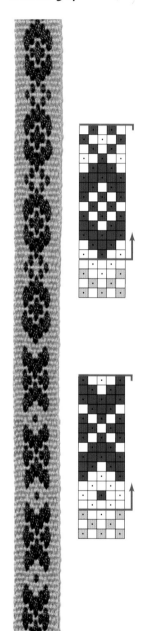

Continuous pattern

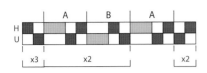

Warp: 3x2/16, indigo and pink
Weft: 3x2/16, indigo

Baltic-5 5

Baltic-5 6

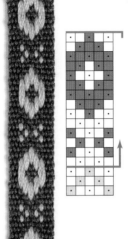

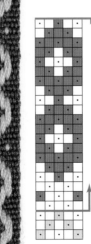

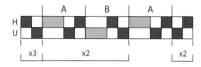

Warp: 3x2/16, indigo and pink
Weft: 3x2/16, indigo

Baltic-5 7

Baltic-5 8

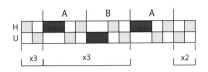

x3   x3   x2

Warp: 3x2/16, yellow and indigo
Weft: 3x2/16, yellow

Baltic-7 1

Baltic-7 2

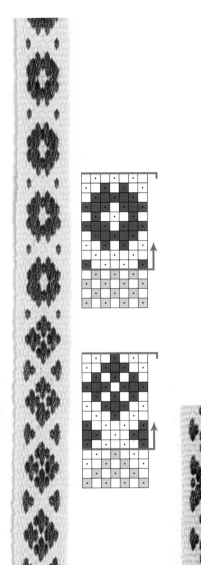

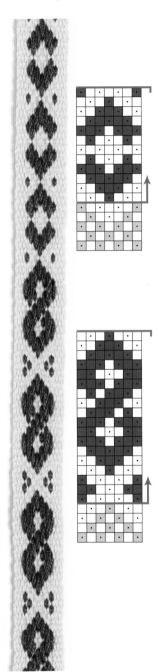

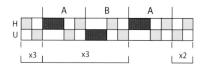

Warp: 2/16, yellow and indigo

Weft: 2/16, yellow

Baltic-7 3

Baltic-7 4

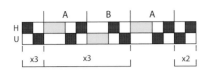

Warp: 3x2/16, indigo and yellow
Weft: 3x2/16, indigo

Baltic-7 5

Baltic-7 6

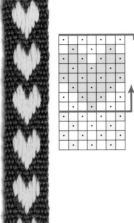

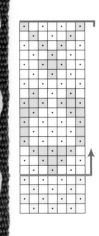

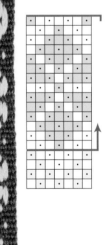

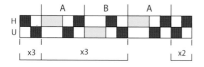

Warp: 2/16, indigo and yellow
Weft: 2/16, yellow

Baltic-7 7

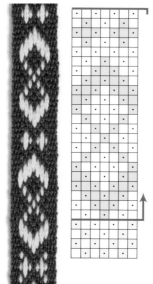

Baltic-7 8

The reverse pattern is exactly the same as the front.

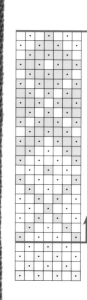

Again, the reverse is exactly the same as the front.

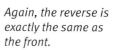

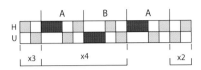

Warp: 3x2/16, pale blue and indigo

Weft: 3x2/16, pale blue

Baltic-9 1

Baltic-9 2

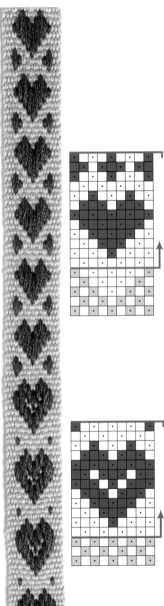

Baltic-Style 9

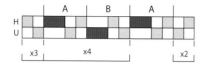

Warp: 2/16, pale blue and indigo
Weft: 2/16, pale blue

Baltic-9 3

Baltic-9 4

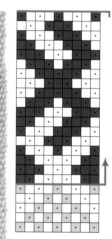

Both pattern threads and background show the same image.

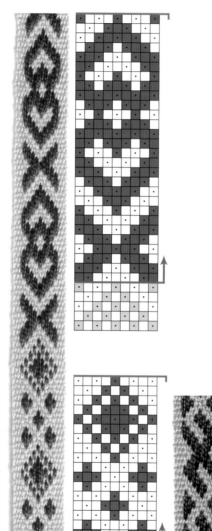

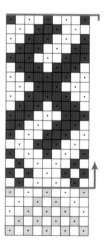

Again, both pattern threads and background show the same image.

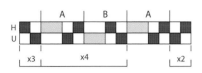

Warp: 3x2/16, indigo and pale blue

Weft: 3x2/16, indigo

Baltic-9 5

Baltic-9 6

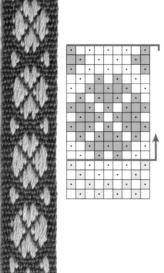
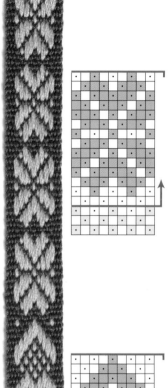

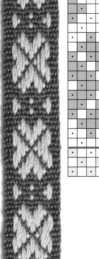
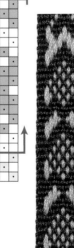

Baltic-Style 9

Warp: 2/16, indigo and pale blue
Weft: 2/16, indigo

Baltic-9 7

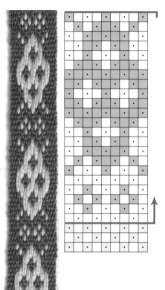

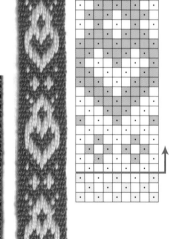

Baltic-9 8

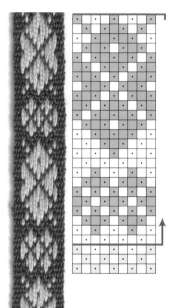

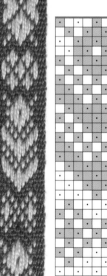

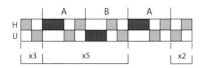

Warp: 2/16, lime and indigo

Weft: 2/16, lime

Baltic-11 1

Baltic-11 2

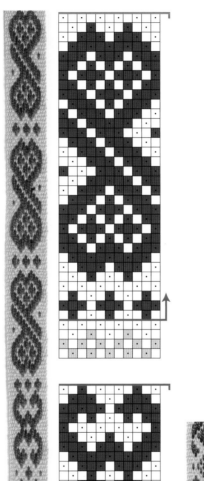

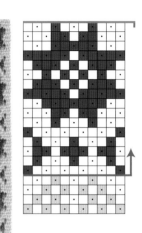

Baltic-Style 11

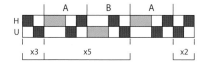

Warp: 2/16, indigo and lime

Weft: 2/16, indigo

Baltic-11 3

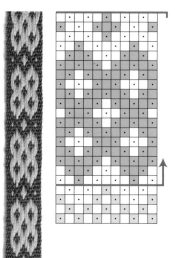

Baltic-11 4

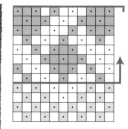

This pattern is much easier to work as shown, with the braided effect appearing on the reverse side.

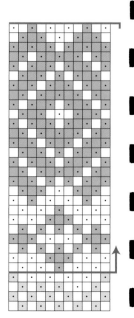

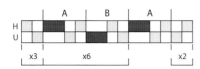

Warp: 2/16, cream and indigo

Weft: 2/16, cream

Baltic-13 1

Baltic-13 2

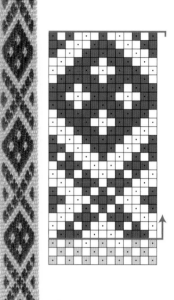

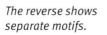

The reverse shows separate motifs.

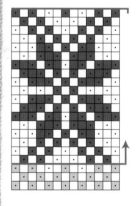

Baltic-13 3

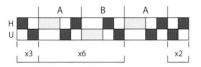

Warp: 2/16, indigo and cream
Weft: 2/16, indigo

Baltic-13 4

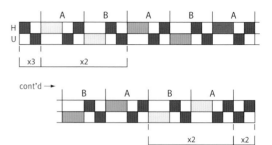

Warp: 2/16, indigo, cream, rust, and orange
Weft: 2/16, indigo

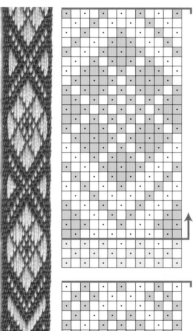
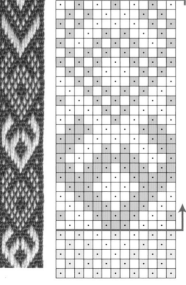
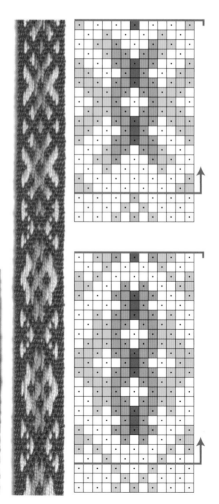

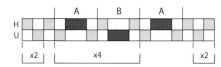

Warp: 3x2/16, indigo and pale blue
Weft: 3x2/16, pale blue

The reverse image is not shown because lettering is one-sided and every combination of letters creates its own layout.

Baltic Lettering 1

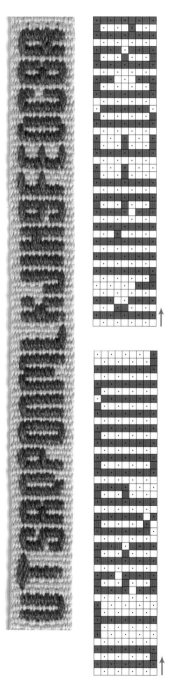

Baltic Lettering 2

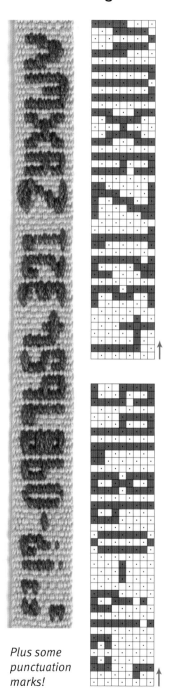

Plus some punctuation marks!

Lettering on Baltic-Style 5 Threading

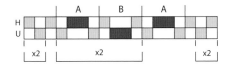

Warp: 3x2/16, pink and indigo

Weft: 3x2/16, pink

The reverse image is not shown because lettering is one-sided and every combination of letters creates its own layout.

Baltic Lettering 3

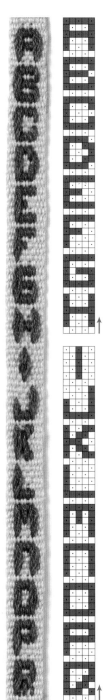

Baltic Lettering 4

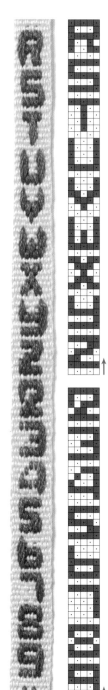

The numeral 1 is not shown—use the letter I instead.

Designing Baltic patterns

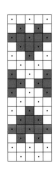

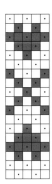

Use a square pattern chart the same width as the number of pattern threads.

The pattern can repeat in short lengths or several patterns over an extended length. Use the dotted Baltic-design chart on page 169.

The dots show where the pattern thread is naturally in the upper level of the shed, the empty (white) squares show where the pattern threads are naturally in the lower level of the shed in that pick.

Impose your design on this grid by shading in squares. Squares with dots that are shaded represent naturally raised pattern threads that need to remain in the upper level of the shed; those with uncolored dots are to be dropped down.

Floats are best started and finished at a dot. One dot to the next creates a vertical float of 3; if the float is extended to the next vertical dot, the float will extend over 5. Instead of making a float over 7 threads, divide it into two floats of 3 each, with a gap of a naturally lowered pattern thread (white in the chart). Don't forget to check the combined length of floats at the finish and start of the design.

Where floats cross over white squares, the pattern thread will need to be picked up.

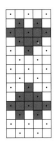

When the main pattern has been inserted, check the vertical unshaded lengths. These, too, should be no longer than 5 as unshaded squares represent a float on the reverse. Finally, check the combined float length at the finish and start of the design.

If there are unshaded lengths of more than 5, create a small motif to fill the gaps. This could be as small as a single naturally raised dot.

Other filler motifs, such as diagonals and crosses, are useful to regulate the pattern structure. Sometimes the repeat of the main design can be moved two or more rows apart to create a better space for the filler design.

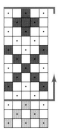

Breaking the rules: I've never seen these rules written down anywhere. They are what I have deduced from studying original pattern bands. For the most part, they make a successful band more likely, but with care they can be disregarded.

No floats over more than 5 wefts: Exercise caution if you really feel that a longer float is necessary for your design. Remember that longer floats can catch on things; an overlong float slips out of place rather easily. If too many long floats are made using the same pattern thread, that warp thread can become loose, as it is not interweaving with the weft as often as the other warp threads. Extra-long floats are best used only with very fine threads.

Start and finish at a dotted square: The reason for this rule is that it is the easiest way to weave; however, the design may demand that this rule is broken. Raised threads started between dots are not always as neat as those started on dots.

The weft must be same color as the background threads: The reason for this rule is that a different-colored weft, showing as small spots, could distract from the main pattern. However, with care, a subtle difference between background warp and weft color can sometimes be successful. Experiment with different weft colors at the end of a warp.

Remember, if you want the weft to be hidden, the selvedge must be the same color. You can use as many pattern threads as you wish. Some beautiful Lithuanian sashes are woven with more than fifty pattern threads. Alternatively, place a wide pattern within borders of two narrower Baltic-pattern bands. Other techniques can also be used as borders, or the Baltic pattern can be used as a border for another technique.

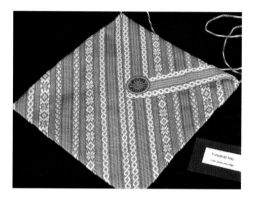

Inkles can be stitched together to create wider fabric suitable for bags because it is so sturdy. This clutch was made by the author using Baltic-style bands.

South American Pebble Weave

Although this technique can be seen on bands from many countries around the world, it is in the South American countries that the most elaborate designs are found.

Several different names have been given to this technique, such as diamond background, reticulated, Bolivian pebble, and Peruvian pebble. The pebble is formed by the thick pattern threads appearing on alternate picks, while the finer background thread is forced to zigzag around them, appearing as diamonds.

This technique has many similarities to basic pick-up from unheddled threads, but in addition to picking up pattern threads, some are also dropped down out of their normal row.

Warping for South American pebble is very specific. In the pattern area, the warp threads are one fine heddled background thread, followed by repeats of doubled thick unheddled pattern threads. The sequence of doubled pattern thread/background thread is repeated as often as required. Many of the traditional designs have a sequence of eleven or twenty-one pattern threads, with delightful short three-pattern-thread designs used as borders. Other numbers are also used.

The pattern threads must be thicker than the background threads and are usually doubled, with two threads working as one. Doubling the threads means that they can spread outward when floating. The weft needs to be exactly the same as the fine background thread in the warp, as the interaction of weft and background warp forms the diamonds.

Warping chart example:

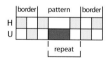

NOTE:

The borders can be as wide as required, but should be about a minimum of six threads on each side to stabilize the weaving.

The thick pattern thread is denoted by a wide rectangle.

The pattern area includes the finer heddled threads on either side of the doubled thick pattern threads.

The number of times the pair of thick pattern and fine background threads is to be repeated is indicated in the charts for the samples.

The nature of the pattern thread will be stipulated at the top of each sample strip.

Weaving

The pattern threads and background threads are raised alternately. The sheds are referred to according to which type of thread is raised to the top layer before any manipulation.

Do not use the weft to draw the warp threads too closely together, or the diamond patterning and other spacing will be obscured. It can be helpful to fan out the heddled threads on the top peg slightly. The weft will show in this technique—it is meant to!

A good firm beat is best for pebble weave, so that the pebbles appear as separate small round bumps on the alternate picks. Practice weaving the background first.

To weave the pebble background (this is worked when the pattern threads are raised):

Note the diamond background and the small alternating and separate pebbles.

Raise the pattern threads.

Drop alternate pattern threads.

Weave the pick, change, tug, beat.

Weave the background pick, change, tug, beat.

Drop the opposite alternate pattern threads.

Weave the pick, change, tug, beat.

Weave the background pick, change, tug, beat.

To weave the pattern area (worked when the background threads are raised):

Raise the background threads.

Pick up and add the alternate pattern threads that were raised in the previous pick.

Weave the background pick, change, tug, beat.

Weave this shed with *all* the pattern threads raised; change, tug, beat.

Pick up and add the opposite alternate pattern threads.

Weave the pick, change, tug, beat.

Weave the pattern pick with *all* the pattern threads raised; change, tug, beat.

Note how the pattern threads spread out over the background:

Reading the pattern charts

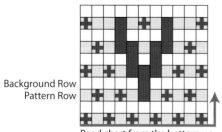

Background Row
Pattern Row

Read chart from the bottom up.

⊞ Pattern thread that remains up on a pattern row.

■ Pattern thread raised on a pattern or background row.

▢ Pattern thread pushed down on a pattern row.

▢ Pattern thread down on a background row.

Only pattern threads are shown on the chart. (Remember, if the pattern threads consist of doubled threads, then two work together as one and are represented by a single square on the chart.)

The lightly shaded rows are where the pattern threads would normally be raised. If a square is colored or contains a colored cross, the pattern thread it represents remains up; if a square is uncolored, the pattern thread should be dropped down.

White rows indicate where the background threads are naturally raised. However, they *do not* represent individual background threads; instead they represent pattern threads in the lower level of the shed. A pattern thread to be picked up on a background row will be shaded in, with the shading continuing from a previously raised pattern thread.

With the woven grid forming the motif on the upper surface, the same motif will theoretically appear as a pebbled motif underneath, but the reverse pattern is not always as clear.

Traditional patterns include a wide range of designs, including plants and flowers, geometric designs, animals, and people.

Reverses

These are not shown, as the pattern clarity is not usually as good on the underside.

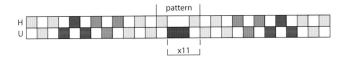

Warp: pattern doubled, 3x2/16, brown

Borders and background: 2/16, cream, tan, orange

Weft: 2/16, cream

11 Pattern Threads 1

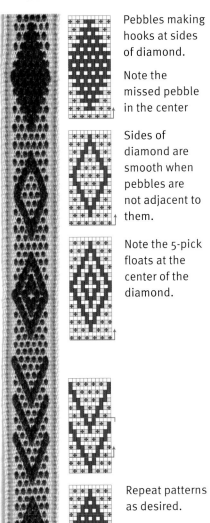

Pebbles making hooks at sides of diamond.

Note the missed pebble in the center

Sides of diamond are smooth when pebbles are not adjacent to them.

Note the 5-pick floats at the center of the diamond.

Repeat patterns as desired.

11 Pattern Threads 2

Small pattern to place between motifs.

Repeat leaves and fronds as required.

Small pattern to place between motifs.

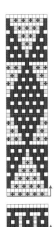

Repeat as required.

Small pattern to place between motifs.

Individual, 11 Pattern Threads

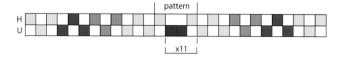

Warp: pattern doubled, 3x2/16, brown

Borders and background: 2/16, cream, tan, orange

Weft: 2/16, cream

11 Pattern Threads 3

Small pattern to place between motifs.

One variation of this frequent motif of a girl/woman with elaborate head-dress.

Small pattern to place between motifs.

11 Pattern Threads 4

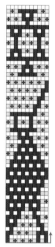

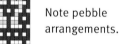

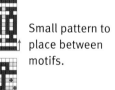

Flower and bird.

Note missing pebbles.

Note pebble arrangements.

The reverse shows an equally intricate design.

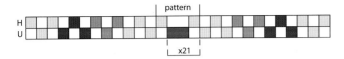

Warp: pattern doubled,
3x2/16, red

Borders and background:
2/16, cream, tan, brown

Weft: 2/16, cream

21 Pattern Threads 1

21 Pattern Threads 2

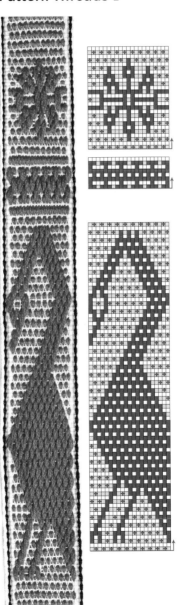

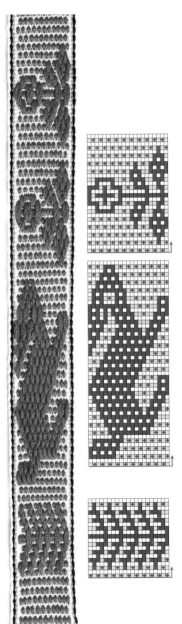

Individual, 21 Pattern Threads

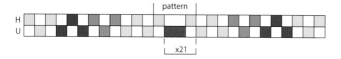

Warp: pattern doubled, 3x2/16, red

Borders and background: 2/16, cream, tan, brown

Weft: 2/16, cream

21 Pattern Threads 3

21 Pattern Threads 4

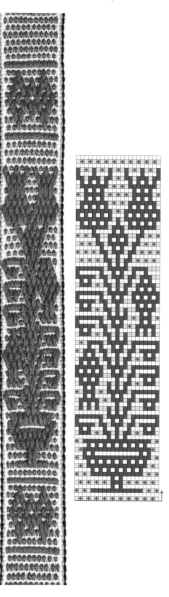

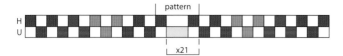

NOTE: *Yellow has been used to represent cream for clarity*

Warp: pattern doubled, 3x2/16, cream

Borders and background: 2/16, brown, tan, red

Mirror Images 1

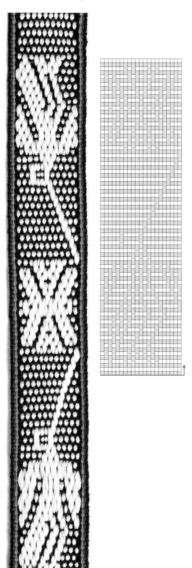

Mirror Images 2

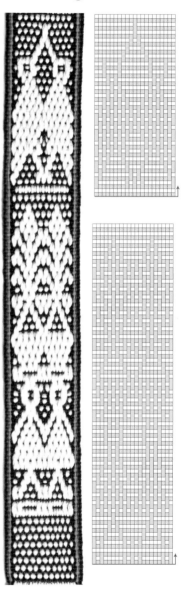

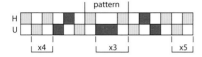

Warp: pattern doubled, 3x2/16, red
Borders and background: 2/16, cream, red
Weft: 2/16, cream

Note the position of the fine red threads, which match the color of the pattern threads.

A different color than the pattern thread color could be used, although this would alter the overall appearance of the pattern.

These narrow patterns are frequently used as the borders for wider patterns.

3 Pattern Threads 1

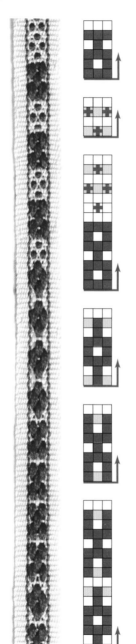

3 Pattern Threads 2

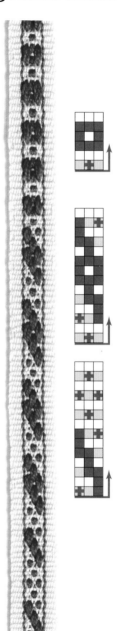

Paired pebbles

A less well-known technique than the usual South American pebble weave, pairs of pebbles (as the name suggests) are always worked together, with the same pairing throughout. The same warping draft is used as for South American pebbles, double-thick pattern threads on the unheddled (U) row alternating with fine background threads in a contrasting color on the heddled (H) row, but here, an even number of thicker pattern threads are worked in pairs. An odd number of pairs is usual.

Pebbles and grids of floats appear on the surface of paired pebble weave, but the finer background threads do not form a diamond net, and the areas of raised threads are bold and clear:

The pebble sequence is formed by dropping down alternate pairs of pattern threads on alternate pattern rows.

Because the pairs of warp pattern threads are always worked together, they expand to cover the same area as a single pick, so the pattern chart is a square grid, with each square representing a *pair* of warp pattern threads and a single row (pick):

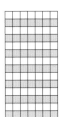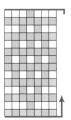

Alternate rows are shaded to represent the naturally raised warp threads.

When pairs of pattern threads are lifted together, the weft floats underneath the inkle over 5 threads at that point. Although there is a little distortion, it is largely counteracted by the adjacent threads.

Similar patterns can be made to those in the usual South American pebble, but obviously, twice as many threads are needed.

To weave Paired Pebble patterns:

Drop down those pairs of pattern threads not needed on the pattern row.

On the heddled (unshaded) row, pick up the pairs of pattern threads required for each pick. Pairs of pattern threads are picked up only from those threads that were not dropped down on the previous pattern (unheddled) row.

The pattern chart again shows the unheddled row as a shaded row. The blank (white) squares show where the pairs of pattern warps are dropped down. They *do not* represent the background threads.

Floats can be over 3 or 5, on both the upper and lower surfaces.

Reverses

Reverses are shown with this technique, as the reverse often shows an equally effective, different design.

Paired Pebbles

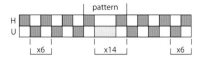

Warp: 2/16, orange; pattern warp 3x2/16, cream

Weft: 2/16, orange throughout

Paired 1

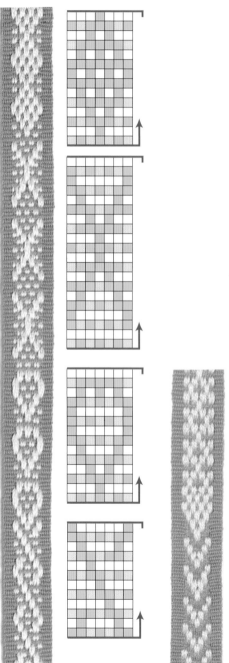

Paired 2

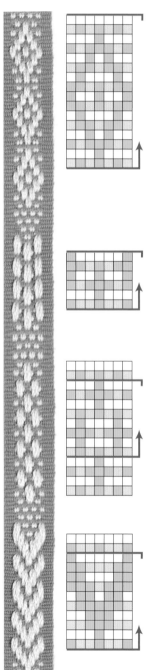

Designing South American pebbles

Use the design chart on page 170. Use a width matching the number of pattern threads. *Only* the pattern threads are used on the chart, as the diamond background forms automatically.

Every alternate row on the chart is lightly shaded to represent an unheddled row of pattern threads. The pick-up rows are the heddled rows and are left empty.

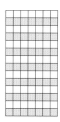

Floats are always made from one shaded square to the next one above or below (three in a vertical line) and thus float over 3, or occasionally 5, picks.

Geometric designs are based on diagonals or blocks.

To make a diagonal

Pattern row (shaded): Start on a shaded pattern row and color in alternate squares.

Pick-up row: Choose one of the preceding colored squares and color from that to the square in the next shaded row.

Pattern row: In the next pattern row, color the squares that were not colored in the preceding shaded pattern row.

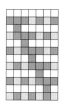

Note: Where the float finishes, three adjacent pattern squares will be colored.

Pick-up row: Begin a new float by coloring one of the squares on one side of the previous float and extend it to the next pattern row.

Continue in this way and a diagonal or zigzag line will emerge.

Color in alternating squares remaining on each pattern row for the pebbles. Those squares not colored in represent the pattern threads to be dropped down.

Blocks of floats

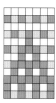

More than one float can be made at a time. Normally the floats will be made with alternate pattern threads.

Lightly create an outline of a shape on the design chart and fill with alternating floats from shaded row to shaded row.

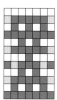

Fill in the background with pebbles.

The first (lower) row can be entirely filled in, if you wish, to create a straight edge.

You can keep the order of the pebbles in a consistent alternating sequence throughout the design, in which case you will notice that the lower diagonals have no pebbles next to them and consequently present a clear line.

Or you can fit in the pebbles to suit, making sure that there are no uncolored vertical lines longer than five, as the pattern thread will float under the inkle at this point.

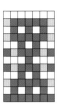

Designing paired pebbles

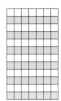

Most of the time the pebbles, those pattern threads in the background left above the inkle in the pattern rows, will be placed alternately on sequential pattern rows. Maintain this alternating sequence as much as possible, but if it is necessary to disrupt the sequence, try to place the pebbles that are directly above each other where there are only a few pebbles, to make the dislocation less obvious.

If you want to keep the sides of the diagonal free from pebbles on its edges, either rearrange the pebbles or, if that is not possible because other blocks of floats also require pebbles in a particular place, drop 2 adjacent pattern threads at that point next to the diagonal.

The design chart looks the same as that for South American pebble, but remember that each square represents one pair of pattern threads, and the same two threads are used as a pair throughout the weaving.

As the pattern threads are already used in consistent pairs, it is unwise to pick up adjacent floats as then the weft will be floating under nine threads at that point.

Keep to simple shapes as this technique creates very clear designs.

Pebbles can be repositioned in sequence to fit in with the blocks of floats, but again make sure that there are no vertical lines of uncolored squares greater than five in total.

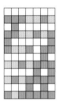

Both these manipulations of design can be seen on traditional South American woven bands, but you often have to look carefully to notice them.

Do not have more than two adjacent floats on a pick-up row or more than two adjacent unmarked squares on a pattern row.

The areas of floats dominate the pebble background.

Monk's Belt

The monk's belt technique is said to have taken its name from the small geometric patterns on a monk's belt.

Traditionally monk's belt is woven as a balanced tabby weave on a 4-shaft loom with a thick pattern weft floating in blocks above and below the fabric. It can be turned, rotated 90 degrees, so that wefts become warps and vice versa. When monk's belt is turned on a 4-shaft loom, the floats are made by a thick pattern warp threaded on two shafts, which alternate with fine warp threads on the other two shafts that weave the tabby background.

When transferring this technique to the inkle loom, it is necessary for the finer background threads to be warped as heddled and unheddled alternately, so that they always weave tabby, with the pattern warp threads between them.

All the pattern threads are warped as heddled threads, one on either side of a finer heddled background thread. This helps to keep them in the right order and makes the manipulation technique consistent. An added advantage is that having three heddled threads adjacent to each other helps to keep the background tabby slightly apart, although it also means that the weft should be the same color as the background tabby threads because it will show slightly.

The warping draft is made up of repeats of one un-heddled background thread followed by three heddled threads: a pattern thread, a background thread, and a second pattern thread.

There will always be an even number of thick pattern warp threads.

Reading the pattern charts

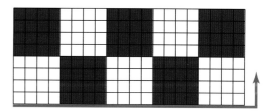

Read the chart from the bottom up.
Each square represents one pattern thread and one row.

■ Pattern thread picked up on a row.

□ Pattern thread dropped down on a row.

The patterns are shown on squared paper, each square representing one warp pattern thread and one row.

Read the charts upward, in the direction in which you weave.

Weaving monk's belt patterns

Open the heddled shed, beat.

Place first two fingers of each hand into the shed and drop down those pattern threads not required.

Beat this new shed again, tug, weave.

Open the unheddled shed, beat.

Place the first two fingers of each hand into the shed.

Pick up pattern threads required.

Beat this new shed again, tug, weave.

Repeat this sequence.

It helps to push the shuttle hard against the fell when beating after the pattern threads have been selected and then to rock the shuttle up and down a few times.

Reverses

The reverse sides are shown because, depending on the pattern, they may be either very different or, sometimes, even identical to the upper face.

Monk's Belt

Pattern threads: 3x2/16, purple

Tabby ground: 2/16, pale sage

Weft: 2/16, pale sage

Alternating Blocks 1

Alternating Blocks 2

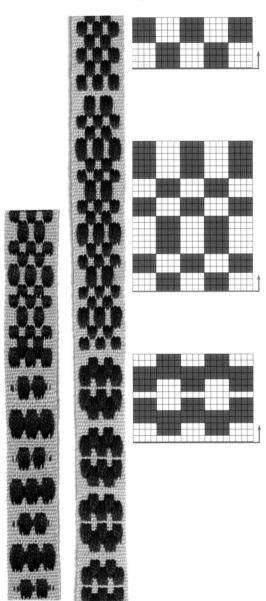

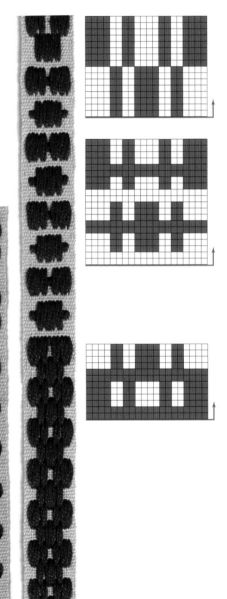

Monk's Belt

Pattern threads: 3x2/16, purple

Tabby ground: 2/16, pale sage

Weft: 2/16, pale sage

Petite

Floribunda

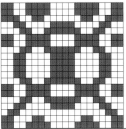

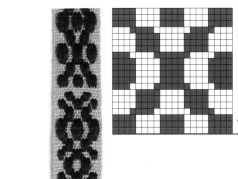

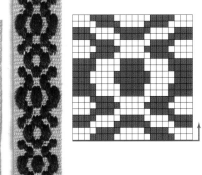

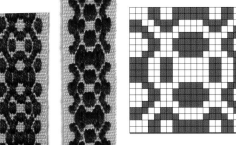

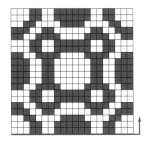

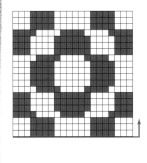

Monk's Belt

Pattern threads: 3x2/16, purple
Tabby ground: 2/16, pale sage
Weft: 2/16, pale sage

Small Honeysuckle

Leaf Line

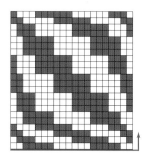

Pattern makes an S diagonal.

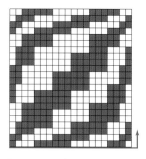

Pattern makes a Z diagonal.

Patterns may be repeated and combined as desired.

Note that the reverse is identical to the face.

Pattern threads: 3x2/16, purple

Tabby ground: 2/16, pale sage

Weft: 2/16, pale sage

Flower, Heart, Butterfly

Flower

Heart and reverse

Butterfly

Monk's Belt

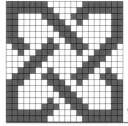

Pattern threads: 3x2/16, purple
Tabby ground: 2/16, pale sage
Weft: 2/16, pale sage

Josephine Knots are woven of combinations of five pattern segments. For each knot, weave the sequence of pattern segments in the order given below. (Where a segment's letter is followed by X and a number, repeat that segment the number of times indicated.) Remember to read the charts upward.

Knot 3 (Third knot from bottom):
Weave A, B, C, D.

Knot 2 (Second knot from bottom):
Weave A, BX2, C, D.

Knot 1 (Bottom knot):
Weave A, BX3, C, M, BX2, C, D

Knotwork

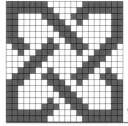

Solomon's Knot

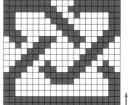

Foundation Celtic Knots

D

C

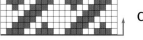

B

A

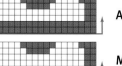

M

Josephine Knots

Designing monk's belt

Monk's belt is very simple to design, provided you follow the basic rules.

Use squared paper. Patterns must always be an even number of squares in the width. You can extend the width and length of the pattern as far as you want. Each square represents one warp pattern thread.

The warp floats may be longer than usual, especially when several floats are adjacent to each other, but do check that the horizontal lengths of unfilled squares (which form floats on the reverse side) do not have too many.

As many warp pattern threads can lie adjacent to each other as you wish. However, except when they are part of a preceding or subsequent float, individual pattern threads in a row do not work very well. For clarity, use at least two adjacent pattern threads in a row.

The weft thread will show a little because of the crowded threading of the three adjacent heddled warp threads.

The reverse of the pattern is also usually interesting. In fact, the pattern on the reverse is often as pleasing as the one on the face.

Use the warping draft chart on page 167: a fine unheddled ground thread followed by three heddled threads (a thick pattern thread, a fine ground thread, a thick pattern thread).

Krokbragd

Krokbragd is a Scandinavian weft-faced weave on three shafts using three shuttles. By turning the weave draft, it becomes a warp-faced weave that uses only one shuttle; however, three sheds (separate layers of warp) are needed to weave it.

The three shed layers are warped in sequence with the first heddled and then two as unheddled threads. Once the warp has been made, the two unheddled shed layers must be separated so that they can be individually raised in their correct sequence.

Warping

The warping draft below shows the three separate rows of warp. These are labeled H1 (Heddled row 1), U2 and U3 (Unheddled rows 2 and 3). The sheds are identified by the row of warp that forms the upper layer of the shed.

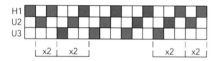

The numbers in brackets under the draft show how many times to repeat each threading section.

Reading from the left, warp the threads in the correct sequence, placing heddles on the heddled-layer threads as you wind in the usual manner, and except for the first and last sections, winding two unheddled threads, which will form the second and third shed layers in between each heddled thread. Note that only one unheddled thread is placed in the sections at the beginning and end of the warp, because both un-heddled rows will raise these threads. After the warp is wound, controls for the unheddled rows are made.

To make the auxiliary heddle for the U3 warp threads, you will need extra heddles, one fewer than the number used already, and a large safety pin or metal knitting stitch holder to hold them together.

When the warp has been wound, place auxiliary loops on the U3 threads. For these, it is easiest to use spare heddles of the normal type for your loom. Working from the upper surface of the warp, separate the heddled threads in turn to expose the unheddled threads and loop a heddle around the U3 thread lying between them. You will also need to place auxiliary heddles on the outermost U2 warp threads in the sections at the beginning and end (these have no U3 next to them). The loose ends of the heddles should extend above the warp. Place the loose ends of each heddle in turn onto the large safety pin or stitch holder.

Behind the heddled threads is best but if the space between the top peg and the joining peg is short, then put the auxiliary heddles in front of the normal heddles.

For the shed stick that controls the U2 row, you will need a short flat stick with a hole at each end. Tie a short length of thread, about 12" (30.5 cm) long into one of the holes. Using the shed stick, and working behind the heddles, put the end of the shed stick without the thread under each U2 warp thread in turn and over each U3 warp thread in turn (the U3 threads are the ones already looped with heddles). Remember to include the U2 warp threads at the beginning and end under the stick as well. When all of the second layer of warp threads are in place, take the length of thread above the heddled threads and tie it into the other hole, so that the stick is under the second warp layer.

Making the sheds

Each warp layer can be placed uppermost independently. To have the heddled threads (H1) uppermost, merely push down the unheddled threads in the usual way.

position of auxiliary heddles
for U3 warp ends

position of shed stick
(under U2 warp ends)

■ U2 Unheddled warp ends ■ U3 Unheddled warp ends
(H1 Heddled warp ends not shown)

To lift U2, lift the shed stick above the other unheddled threads, placing the fingers of one hand in the gap to assist, and confirm the shed by placing your other hand in the shed in front of the heddles.

To lift U3, pull the auxiliary heddles up and confirm the shed as previously described. If this proves difficult, because the inkle is wide or the threads cling together, then place a second group of auxiliary heddles on the U2 threads (those on the shed stick) but with the heddles and a safety pin hanging below the weaving next to the auxiliary heddles on U3. By pulling the U3 layer up and the U2 layer down simultaneously, a good shed will be produced.

Weaving

The first warp layer (H1) is uppermost every alternate pick; the second (U2) and third (U3) layers are uppermost at intervals of 4 picks, alternately in between the first layer. So the shed sequence is: 1, 2, 1, 4, repeat. To weave this sequence:

Push U2 and U3 down for H1.

Lift U2.

Push U2 and U3 down for H1.

Lift U3.

Repeat.

The outermost unheddled threads at either end of U2 are also raised when U3 is the upper layer. This is to control the tendency of the edges of the inkle to curl upward if the layers are all entirely separate.

On the back, the H1 shed weaves tabby as usual; however, the U2 and U3 warp layers each float for 3 picks, showing as blocks of floats that cover the tabby threads between.

Starting and finishing

As usual:

It is neater to start and finish with a 4-pick krokbragd sequence:

If you start with an ordinary heddled versus unheddled sequence, weave four picks before starting the krokbragd sequence. The warp threads in these 4 picks will not show the pattern. If the finish is made as a heddled versus unheddled sequence, however, the last unheddled layer will dominate the last 4 picks.

Reverses

Reverses are shown. Notice the 3-pick floats of U2 and U3 warps that appear on this side.

Pebbles

Warp: 3x2/16, medium green, yellow, and navy

Weft: 3x2/16, medium green

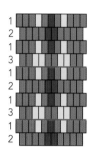

Circles and Ovals

cont'd →

Warp: 3x2/16, medium green, red, and navy

Weft: 3x2/16, medium green

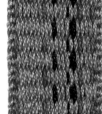

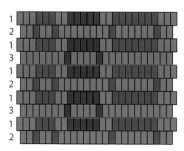

Single, Double, and Triple Overlap Events

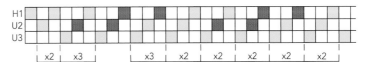

H1																														
U2																														
U3																														

x2 x3   x3 x2 x2 x2 x2 x2

cont'd →

x3 x3 x2

Warp: 3x2/16, yellow and medium green

Weft: 3x2/16, yellow

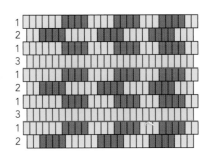

Long and Short Lengths, Uneven

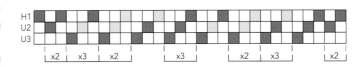

H1																														
U2																														
U3																														

x2 x3 x2   x3   x2 x3   x2

Warp: 3x2/16, medium green, yellow

Weft: 3x2/16, medium green

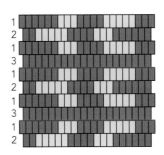

Krokbragd

Single Flowers

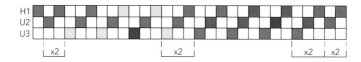

Warp: 3x2/16, medium green, yellow, red, and blue

Weft: 3x2/16, medium green

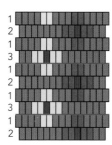

Flower Border

Warp: 3x2/16, medium green, yellow, red, and blue

Weft: 3x2/16, medium green

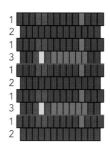

Krokbragd

Zigzags, Single, Double, and Triple Overlaps, Uneven and Even

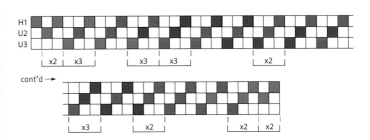

H1
U2
U3

x2 | x3 | x3 | x3 | x2

cont'd →

x3 | x2 | x2 | x2

Warp: 3x2/16, medium green, red, and navy

Weft: 3x2/16, medium green

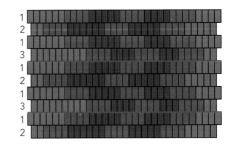

1
2
1
3
1
2
1
3
1
2

Traditional

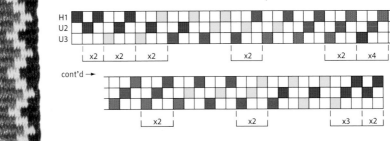

H1
U2
U3

x2 | x2 | x2 | x2 | x2 | x4

cont'd →

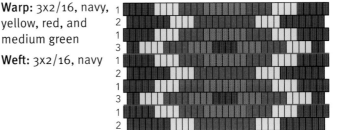

x2 | x2 | x3 | x2

Warp: 3x2/16, navy, yellow, red, and medium green

Weft: 3x2/16, navy

1
2
1
3
1
2
1
3
1
2

Designing Krokbragd

Designing is done on the same design sheet used for basic color patterns. The krokbragd repeat, however, is over 4 picks, and the first and third pick must be the same.

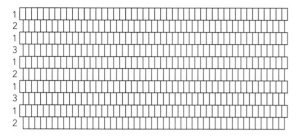

A red horizontal line separates the complete design repeat of four sheds.

Designing with krokbragd means that you can create isolated patterns rather than the linked basic color patterns. Like basic color patterns, krokbragd patterning is fixed according to the order of the warp threads, but several patterns can be adapted, extended, or combined.

When I was making the sample for the top of page 107, I made a mistake, which resulted in a new design idea. My mistake was to repeat the first part of the sequence: 1, 2, 1, 2, 1, 3. Of course, this meant even longer floats over five picks at the back, but the effect was exciting. So here is a short sample showing deliberate out-of-order sequences (no longer a mistake but a pattern!). Try this idea with other patterns, making your own sequences. Five picks is probably as long as you should make unless the inkle is to be stitched to something. The warp threads of the missed layers would also become slacker than the rest.

An inkle worked in krokbragd is thicker and firmer than normal, making it ideal for items such as bags, bag handles, and belts.

The bag on page 109 is worked in 2-ply rug yarn (see page 109). (It needed those extra pull-down auxiliary heddles!) The pattern is Japanese *furoshiki*. The length must be three times the width and then is folded this way.

With wrong side up, fold the lower left corner to meet the top.

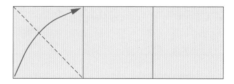

Fold the portion at the right to match the first fold.

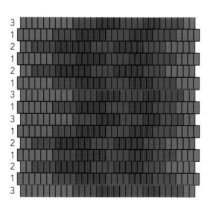

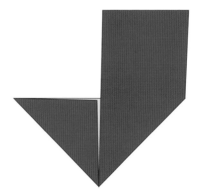

Turn over and fold the top corner down to the center.

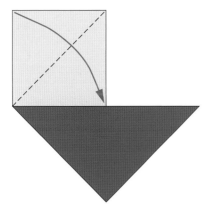

Stitch the edges together where they meet.

The body of the bag is woven in four separate krok-bragd strips with the same color at the edges, which meant that when handsewn together, with the same thread and color as the outer warp threads, the stitching does not show.

The handle is woven in yet another krokbragd strip.

The fringes at the ends of the strips are sandwiched between two strips of basic color-patterned inkles, which are thinner than the krokbragd strips.

The tie at the center is woven in a tubular technique.

Krokbragd bag with rya muff (see pages 128–129 for the rya technique).

Warp Changes

Changing individual warp threads

Changing warp threads can be understood as changing either the color or type of warp threads.

Clasped warps

In weft-faced weaving, such as floor rugs and tapestry, the technique of clasped wefts is sometimes used to link two different weft threads in the same or adjoining picks.

The same principle can be used to link different warp threads as they are warped. The threads need to be doubled. Using any two pegs on the inkle loom that provide the desired length, make a loop of thread from the first peg around the second and back to the first peg; tie securely with long ties. Either hold the long ties at the starting peg or place the loop on the starting peg to anchor it temporarily and pull a second thread through the loop so that the resulting doubled thread passes around your chosen pathway on the inkle loom. Tie the two together at the starting peg using the long ties of the first loop. (If you have placed the first loop onto the starting peg to anchor it, slip the loop off the starting peg before tying them together.) Other loops can be the same length or different. If you want several initial loops to be the same length on the loom, make their initial knots line up. Whether the warp lengths are heddled or unheddled isn't important; what matters is the position of the knots as both heddled and unheddled warp threads advance at the same rate when woven.

Even when weaving a basic tabby pattern, there will be some discrepancy at the color-change point because of the inevitable small differences in tension. If using for warp-manipulated techniques, then the warp threads that are not interweaving at every pick will show an even greater difference.

Direct change

For more precise control of the change from one color or thread to a different one, use the direct-change method.

At the point where you want to change the thread, snip the warp thread some distance beyond the fell. Place a pin horizontally on the woven inkle about 1½" (4 cm) below the fell. Tie one end of the new warp thread to the free end of the old one and use it to ease the new thread along the pathway (through the heddle if applicable) to the starting knots of the main inkle. Tie the new thread to the beginning of the old thread at the starting knots, then tension and wrap the other end around the pin. Only after the inkle has been removed from the loom are the loose ends carefully stitched through a pick at the back of the inkle.

The direct-change method does involve more finishing than the clasped-warp technique but is absolute in accuracy.

Reverses

Reverses are not shown as these changes do not alter the structure.

Clasped Warp 1

Warp: 2/16, all threads doubled, pink, navy; use orange to start

Weft: 2/16, doubled; pink

Warp within oval changing from orange to green.

Clasped Warp 2

Warp: 2/16, all threads doubled, pink, green, to start.

Weft: 2/16, doubled; pink

Doubled Baltic pattern threads changing from green to red (only part of pattern chart shown).

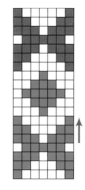

Clasped Warps

Clasped Warp 3

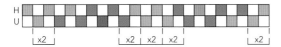

Warp: 2/16 all doubled; pink, green; centers of side patterns change color

Weft: 2/16 doubled; pink

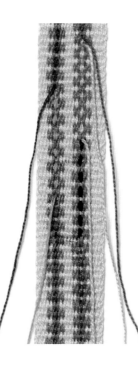

Direct Change

Same warping draft and weft as above.

More frequent changes using pin-and-wrap method.

Some warp threads are left on the surface to show changes, the others have been stitched through the pick.

Additions to the Warp Surface

Auxiliary warp threads

An auxiliary warp thread is one that is added as an extra thread to an already threaded warp. It does not replace any of the existing warped threads.

Auxiliary warp threads can be the same as the existing warp or completely different in thickness and/or texture; they can be started and/or finished where required; they can be heddled or unheddled to fit in with an existing pattern. The auxiliary threads, which can be heddled or unheddled, are placed adjacent to an existing warp thread.

Tied auxiliary warp thread

A tied auxiliary warp thread is tied around the loom, following the same pathway as the rest of the warp. It is inserted either under or over the top peg and knotted as usual at the starting peg. The advantage of the tied method is that a number of auxiliary warp threads can be added, starting and finishing where required, with any loose lengths being inserted into a pick after the inkle is off the loom. The disadvantage is that when the auxiliary threads are used to create surface interest, or are of different fibers, they can become looser than the rest of the tensioned warp.

Free-hanging auxiliary warp thread

A free-hanging auxiliary thread is attached to a weight. The thread passes from the woven inkle either over or under the heddle bar and hangs over the joining peg.

Kumihimo bobbins or small 35mm film canisters weighted with coins are useful as weights because the threads can be wound around them and then let out when the existing warp is advanced around the loom. This is probably the best way to attach auxiliary warp threads, especially when the type of yarn is different or fragile, because the auxiliary thread is tensioned independently; the disadvantage is that more than two or three weights swinging from the joining peg can

destabilize the loom. Make sure that the weights are just heavy enough to fully tension the auxiliary warp thread.

Weighting a free-hanging warp thread

Before inserting a free-hanging auxiliary warp thread, make sure that the starting end is securely fastened to the existing woven inkle, either by inserting the start of the thread through two or more picks and bringing it to the surface where needed or by wrapping the start around a horizontal pin inserted through the woven inkle and stitching the loose thread through the picks after the inkle is removed from the loom. If the auxiliary warp is needed for only a short length, when you are finished weaving with it, cut a little way beyond the fell so that there will be enough yarn either to immediately weave through a few picks or to stitch through a pick after the inkle is removed from the loom.

Method

An auxiliary thread will work with its adjacent existing warp thread unless it is manipulated and held over or under the surface as required. They can be used for ccribbling (see page 119) or to alternate with the existing adjacent warp thread above the inkle every fourth pick (a kind of mini-krokbragd) especially in warp-color pattern and are extremely useful when adding to edges.

Attaching beaded auxiliary warp thread

If possible, the beading yarn should be prethreaded, although additions or changes can be made during weaving. Tie a large slipknot at the end of the thread so it can be pulled open for any rebeading. Then thread the beads in the reverse order from the way you will need them.

Use a beading thread that is as close as possible in color to the existing warp thread with which it is to work. Again, a weighted yarn holder is used; for beading, it is useful if the weight is a small container that that can hold both the beads and yarn. Beads can be released, a few at a time, from the container.

To attach a beading thread, it is best to insert it into its correct place. After making a secure start, weave the thread in for a minimum of three normal weft picks. Three picks are necessary because the beading thread is so very slippery; in addition, they are invisible because the fineness of the beading thread does not alter the nature of the picks. Bring the beading thread to the required position. When weaving in a beading thread, always weave the normal weft through each pick first.

An unheddled beading thread means that you do not have to manipulate the beads through the heddles; they remain just beyond the joining peg and slide down into position only when they are lifted. If used in a heddle, the beads must be manipulated through the heddles, but the beads rest against the heddle and you don't have to reach right behind the loom to bring each bead forward over the joining peg.

The beading thread works together with its adjacent warp thread at all times, unless a bead, or a length of beads needs to float over the surface of the loom for a short length.

An auxiliary beaded warp thread is usually a far neater way to add beads to the warp than weft insertion, although if beads need to be inserted in several vertical locations, a weft-inserted beading thread is preferable (see page 141).

Reverses

Reverse sides are shown to illustrate any floats and to show any alterations to the existing base pattern.

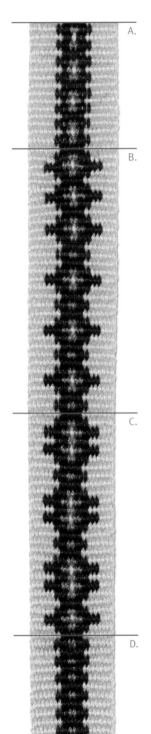

A.

B.

C.

D.

Mini-Krokbragd with Tied Auxiliary Warps

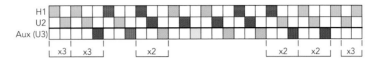

H1																														
U2																														
Aux (U3)																														

x3 x3   x2   x2 x2 x3

Warp: 3x2/16, pink, purple, green, and yellow

Weft: 3x2/16, pink

Warp H1 and U2 only. Add tied auxiliary threads from U3 in correct positions.

A. Tie in yellow from U3. Weave 1-2-1-3.

B. Tie in green threads from U3.
Weave 1-2-1-3.

C. Add remaining purple U3 threads. Weave 1-2-1-3. Experiment with other sequences, e.g., 1-2-1-3-1-2 and 1-2-1-3-1-3-1-2.

D. Weave with only H1 and U2
(and no auxiliary threads from U3).

Tied Auxiliary Warps

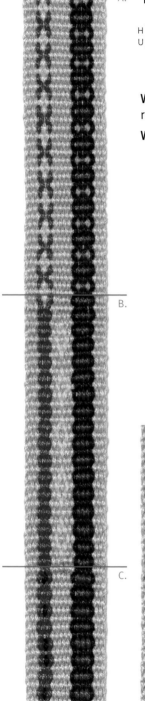

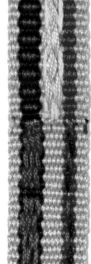

Tied Auxiliary Warps in Stripes

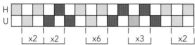

Warp: 3x2/16, pale blue,
red, purple, mauve

Weft: 3x2/16, pale blue

Manipulate all choices by hand.

On the U shed, auxiliary warps (Aux) will rise in a pair with an adjacent unheddled warp thread. Choose either the U warp or the Aux warp from each pair and drop the other. There will be long floats on the back. Remove used Aux warps before installing new ones.

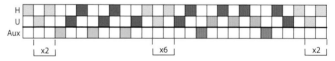

A. Tie in 3 pink threads at center of red and 1 orange on either side of mauve.

B. Tie in 5 yellow threads at center of pale blue.

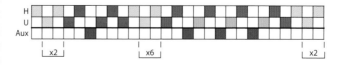

C. Tie in 1 purple thread at center of red and 3 purple threads adjacent to mauve.

A. Hanging Auxiliary Warps

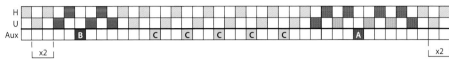

Warp: 3x2/16, pale blue, red, purple, mauve

Weft: 3x2/16, pale blue

A. Space-dyed soft, thick yarn adjoining center mauve thread.

B. Fancy tufted yarn adjoining center red thread.

C. Fine metallic yarns adjoining several threads at center of pale blue group, all hung together on one bobbin.

Baltic-Style

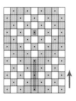

Warp: 2/16, turquoise
Pattern warp: 3x2/16, white
Weft: 2/16, turquoise

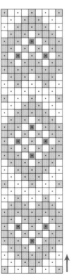

Bead position highlighted on charts.

Scribbling

Imagine filling in a shape by scribbling to and fro with a pencil. That's what scribbling on the inkle loom is—with the inkle being the shape and a pattern-thread warp as the pencil.

The scribbling warp thread, usually a little thicker than the other warp threads, is suspended from the fell of the weaving, adjacent to an unheddled warp thread, and tensioned by a weight beyond the joining peg. See page 113 for the way to secure this auxiliary warp thread.

The scribbling thread remains on the surface at all times and is tied into the weaving at intervals when and where you wish. The scribbling thread can move vertically or at a shallow or steep angle. Two separate scribbling threads can be used.

When the unheddled threads are raised, the scribbling thread is naturally brought above the surface. To keep the scribbling thread on the surface, lift up the scribbling thread before lowering the unheddled threads. To insert the scribbling thread into a new position, take the thread and push a loop of it between two warp threads so that when the next shed is woven the weft thread holds it into position.

When the scribbling thread is not repositioned in any way, it will naturally be inserted below the weft at the next pick where the unheddled threads are lowered. If the scribbles are to return to one position frequently, then it is best to position the auxiliary scribbling thread in that place. If the scribble is to pass backward and forward across the inkle, then it is best to position the auxiliary scribbling thread at the center, even if it is

never going to be inserted at that position.

There are three types of scribble; all can be worked from the side or the center, although random scribbling is probably best worked from a central point.

1. Scribbling thread held down every pick: this type requires careful tugging of the weft so that the scribbling thread doesn't pull the inkle inward.

    For scribble always going from a fixed point, either from the side or center:

    a) Lift the unheddled threads, beat, tug.

    b) Take the scribbling thread to a new position and insert it into the shed between two warp threads.

    c) Weave, taking the weft over the scribbling thread and the heddled threads.

    d) Change the shed, beat, tug, weave (the scribble is held in its natural position).

    For scribble moving randomly across the inkle (position the scribbling thread at the center):

    a) Lift the unheddled threads, beat, tug.

    b) Take the scribbling thread to a new position and insert it into the shed between 2 warp threads.

    c) Weave, taking the weft over the scribbling thread and the heddled threads.

    d) Lift the heddled threads, beat, tug.

e) Take the scribbling thread to a new position and insert it into the shed between 2 warp threads.

f) Weave, taking the weft over the scribbling thread and the unheddled threads.

2. Scribble held down on alternate picks:

For scribble that always goes from a fixed point, either from the side or center:

a) Lift the unheddled threads, beat, tug, weave.

b) Lift up the scribbling thread.

c) Change shed, beat, tug, weave.

d) Change shed, beat, tug.

e) Take the scribbling thread to a new position and insert it into the shed between 2 warp threads.

f) Weave, taking the weft over the scribbling thread and the unheddled threads.

g) Change shed, beat, tug, weave.

h) Change shed, beat, tug, weave (the scribble is in its original position).

For scribble moving randomly across the inkle (position the scribbling thread at the center):

a) Lift the unheddled threads, beat, tug, weave.

b) Lift up the scribbling thread.

c) Change shed, beat, tug, weave.

d) Change shed, beat, tug.

e) Take the scribbling thread to a new position and insert it into the shed between 2 warp threads.

f) Weave, taking the weft over the scribbling thread and the unheddled threads.

3. Scribble held over more than 2 picks. For both return-point scribbling and random:

Weave normally, lifting the scribbling thread as necessary to keep it on the surface and inserting it into new position when required.

Any of the scribbling types can be repeated or combined with one another in a regular or irregular manner.

Two or more separate scribbling threads can be used.

The tied-down scribbling thread only shows as small dots on the reverse of the inkle.

H
U
x31

Warp: 2/16, medium blue

Weft: 2/16, medium blue

Scribble yarn: 3x2/16, in colors indicated below.

Scribbling 1

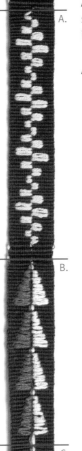

A.

B.

C.

Scribbling on every pick. All these below have the scribbling thread(s) held in the center.

A. Single scribbling thread, yellow, scribbling on alternate picks.

B. Alternating sides; two colors, white and green, each on own side. Decreasing lengths of scribble to form triangles.

C. Varying lengths of scribble; two colors, white and green; increasing and decreasing lengths of scribble to form diamonds, with colors crossing at the center.

Scribbling 2

A.

B.

C.

Single color

A. Single color, pale blue; worked from center; scribbled from side to side in decreasing lengths.

B. Single color, green; worked from side; "Ms and Ws" with scribble worked in a sequence of two short, one long.

C. Two scribbling threads, both pale blue; worked from the center, in opposite directions.

Scribbling

| H |
| U |
| x29 |

Warp: 2/16, medium blue

Weft: 2/16, medium blue

Scribbling 3

A.

B.

C.

Scribbling thread held over 4 picks:

A. Scribbling yarn: green.

B. Two separate scribbling yarns: pale blue and cream.

C. Two separate scribbling yarns: lime and cream.

Scribbling 4

A.

B.

C.

Scribbling yarn held over 5 picks:

A. Scribbling thread: green.

B. Scribbling thread: strung Rocailles 9/0 beads to fit space exactly.

C. Scribbling thread: strung Rocailles 9/0 beads in loops.

Embroidery

Embroidery is worked with a separate embroidery thread that is brought from the back of the inkle to the front, worked over a number of ends or picks, either horizontally, vertically, or diagonally (but not backward), and then stitched down by taking it through to the back again. One or more embroidery threads can be used. By counting the picks and/or ends, it becomes counted-thread embroidery.

The embroidery thread can be a loose or bundled length or wound around a small object such as an EZ-bob. Using an extra shuttle for the embroidery thread can be somewhat clumsy. Start by tying a slipknot, leaving a tail (see page 163) and stitch upward where required. The loose end of the slipknot can be unfastened when the inkle is off the loom and stitched through the back of a pick.

Method

Simple diagonals or verticals can be made by bringing the embroidery thread to the surface, holding it above the warp for a set number of picks, and then reinserting the thread to the back of the inkle.

To make a horizontal line, bring the embroidery thread to the surface and immediately place it back underneath over a number of ends to one side.

For zigzags, first make a diagonal stitch. Keep the shed open and bring the embroidery thread back to the surface to one side and immediately stitch back through the same place as the diagonal finished. Bring the thread to the surface at the same place the horizontal started; change the shed and continue to weave until the embroidery thread needs to be stitched back through the inkle. This will create a double stitch at the back of the inkle.

To make a lazy daisy or detached chain stitch, bring a loop of embroidery thread to the surface and weave several picks. Bring the whole of the embroidery thread to the surface where the daisy petal is to finish, pass it through the loop and adjust the loop to suit, then stitch back through the inkle, either at the same point or after one or two picks.

Two separate embroidery threads are sometimes necessary, either to provide a color variation or because a shape cannot be made with a single thread (see the squares and flowers on page 124).

The floats on the surface (or indeed on the back) should not be too long unless the inkle will be stitched onto something.

Reverses

These are shown because they give an indication of how to work the embroidery and are sometimes interesting in their own right.

Embroidery

One and Two Thread Embroidery 1

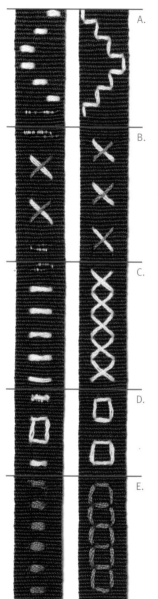

Warp: 2/16, blue

Weft: 2/16, blue

Embroidery wefts: 3x2/16 in colors indicated

A. Single embroidery thread, white; double horizontal stitch on reverse.

B. Two embroidery threads, yellow and green; cross also at back.

C. Two embroidery threads, one color (white); double horizontal stitch on reverse.

D. Squares; two embroidery threads in yellow.

E. Line of squares; two embroidery threads, green; triple horizontal stitches on reverse.

One and Two Thread Embroidery 2

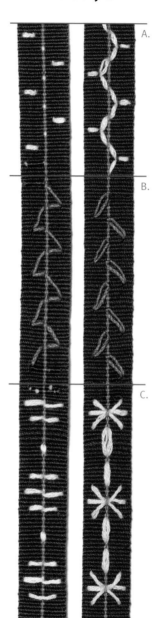

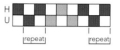

Warp: 2/16, blue and lime green

Weft: 2/16, blue

Embroidery thread: 3x2/16

A. Single embroidery thread, white; double horizontal stitches on reverse.

B. Single embroidery thread, green; lazy daisy stitch.

C. Flowers: 2 white embroidery threads, double horizontal and vertical stitches on reverse.

Soumak and Loops

Both soumak and loops can be worked either with the normal weft thread or with an additional thread. More than one thread can be used in the same shed. Always weave the normal weft first. The additional thread can either be worked from edge to edge or from a position just inside the edges. Bring the soumak or loop thread above the inkle at the beginning of the row, take it below at the end, and move it from underneath the inkle up to the next insertion pick. In the samples, both soumak and loops are worked on an open shed, with the threads forming the soumak manipulated around only the raised warp ends.

Soumak

The soumak thread passes over a number of warp ends in one direction, it's taken back under fewer warp ends, and then is brought to the surface again to continue going over warp ends in the first direction. The instructions say how many raised warp threads to go over and how many to bring it back under. The pathway of a soumak thread can be horizontal (the most usual), diagonal, or vertical. The length of the surface float can be regular or irregular. More than one different soumak thread can be worked in conjunction.

The soumak thread can emerge from below the top float for locked soumak or above it for unlocked soumak. The way it emerges and the direction it is inserted (from the right or left) determines the angle of the crossover of floats. Because soumak is worked first from one side and then from the other, if you want the angle of all the floats to lie in the same direction, it is necessary to change the way the soumak emerges from one row to the next. If the same emerging method is used to work all rows, an attractive V-shaped formation is produced.

Loops

Wrapped loops: If a soumak thread is wrapped around a device such as a knitting needle or dowel as it is brought to the surface, it will create a looped surface float. Wrapped loops can also be taken back over the knitting needle, then down into the shed to make a longer loop and hold the knitting needle in place more securely.

Unwrapped loops are made without taking the thread backward, merely passed over some raised warp ends and then inserted back into the shed to the next position. Unwrapped loops emerging just between warp ends are the least stable of all the knots and are really only suitable for chaining.

Loops can be either left as they are or chained together. If they are to be chained, a crochet hook will simplify the process. Chained loops are made around warps and wefts in much the same way as crochet chains. With a crochet hook, draw up the first loop of thread where desired and size it so that the loop extends to the place where the next loop is to emerge. Insert the hook through the loop and into the shed between two warps at this point and catch the loop weft. Draw up a new loop through both the warp and the previous loop. Repeat as needed for the pattern. The final loop of the chain is held in place by bringing the weft up through the last loop and taking it back into the shed.

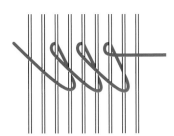

Unlocked Soumak: Emerging thread comes up ABOVE initial float

Emerging thread comes up BELOW initial float

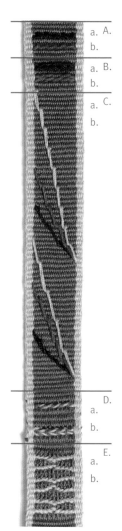

Soumak and Loops 1

Warp: 3x2/16, blue and yellow

Normal Weft: 3x2/16, yellow

Soumak and loop threads: 3x2/16 in colors indicated

Soumak

A. Single rows of soumak
  a) Unlocked soumak from left: over 4, under 2 with navy weft.

  b) Locked soumak from left: over 4, under 2 with red weft.

B. Two soumak rows in the same shed
  a) Unlocked soumak from left, then right: over 6, under 2 (navy weft).

  b) Locked soumak from left, unlocked from right: over 6, under 2 (red weft).

C. Diagonal soumak
  a) Every fourth pick:
  Navy: over 8, under 2.
  Red: over 6, under 2.
  Pale blue: over 4, under 2.

  b) By frequency: all soumak wefts over 6 warps, under 2.
  Navy: every second pick.
  Red: every fourth pick.
  Pale blue: every sixth pick.

D. Additional color (red) with normal weft (yellow) also used for soumak.
  a) Single row alternating over 4, under 2.

  b) Alternating colors:
  Unlocked soumak from left.
  Unlocked from right.

E. Reversing angles of weft spans at center
  a) Using normal (yellow) weft over 2, under 1, reverse soumak direction at center.

  b) Allow one normal pick between each soumak row.

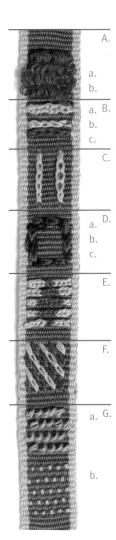

Soumak and Loops 2

Loops

A. Horizontal loops (loop weft: red)
  a) Single row, over 2, under 2.

  b) Alternate picks, over 2, under 2, alternating positions.

B. Horizontal chaining
  a) Over 2, from right (loop weft: yellow).

  b) Over 4, from right (loop weft: pale blue).

  c) Over 4, from left (loop weft: red).

C. Vertical chaining (loop weft: yellow)
  Loop over 2 ends, up every 2 picks.

D. Combined, alternating colors, vertical and horizontal (loop weft: navy and red)
  a) Horizontal between ends every fourth end.

  b) Vertical between ends every other pick.

  c) Horizontal between ends every fourth end.

E. Horizontal chaining, two colors (loop wefts, red and pale blue)
  Between every second end on alternate picks, two loop weft colors in the same shed, brought up as needed.

F. Diagonal chaining (loop wefts: red and normal yellow)
  After the first loops, bring each successive loop up 2 picks and 4 ends to one side. Use one additional color with normal weft.

G. Wrapped loops (loop weft: normal yellow)
  a) Over 2, pass under 4, loops around knitting needle several times.

  b) Small loops pulled tightly to make textured dots.

Turkish and Other Knots

There are different types of knots, but here I have concentrated on three. Do experiment with other types on your own. Any of the surface knots can be combined to create new and interesting surface textures.

Work the knots on a raised shed and insert the normal weft through every pick.

Cut soumak

If a soumak thread is wrapped around a rod and the loops cut afterward, a pile is produced. Because the loops are cut, this cut pile really needs an additional soumak wrap for security. Even so, the stability for this structure is only fair and depends upon how firmly the picks are beaten into place.

Turkish or Ghiordes knot

Knots made with separate short lengths of yarn can be worked in three different ways: locked, unlocked, and sideways. These knots can also be worked with a continuous thread, which is useful when a short pile is required.

Working with separate short lengths

Lengths need to be long enough to manipulate; therefore, a long pile is produced. Several short lengths worked as one will make a thicker pile. The advantage is that all the knots can easily be a uniform size, and the long pile means that the rows of knots can be widely spaced.

To make a locked Turkish knot, the knotting threads need to span at least two warp ends. Bring each short end under and up between the warp ends below the central span, adjust ends to match, and pull downward to the fell of the inkle to fix into position. The pile will lie toward you. Make subsequent rows around alternating pairs of warp ends:

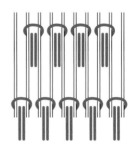

Make an unlocked knot in the same way as the locked knot, but bring up the ends of the knotting threads above the span. The pile will lie away from you:

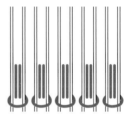

To make a sideways knot, insert the loop under a single warp end in the direction opposite to the direction you want the to go, then bring the ends over and through the loop:

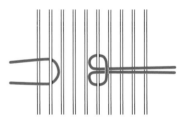

This knot can be thought of as a doubled Turkish knot. Place the knot yarn behind two warp ends; bring the two yarn ends up to the surface. Take each tail of the knot separately over two warp ends, down to the back, and bring each one up between the two warp ends and their floats. This knot is very stable and can lie toward you, away, or even sideways:

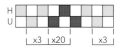

Warp: 3x2/16, medium blue and yellow

Weft: 3x2/16, yellow

Knots: 3x2/16, mixed colors

Turkish and Other Knots 1

A.

B.

C.

D.

E.

F.

A. Rya knots around a rod (looped knotted pile); loop weft: pale blue.

B. Rya knots around a rod and cut (cut pile); pile weft: pale blue.

C. Sideways rya; pile weft: navy.

D. Alternating rya knots, with 1 pick between; pile weft: red.

E. Inserted loops, un-cut; loop weft: green.

F. Inserted loops, cut, 1 pick between; pile weft: green.

Turkish and Other Knots 2

Long rya, 7 picks between, different colors in each row arranged in a pattern sequence.

Inserted Auxiliary Thread Manipulation

Gathering and Pleating

It is very easy to place a gathering or pleating thread into an inkle while it is being woven. Among its advantages over gathering after weaving are that it is far more regular, the inkle's threads are never split by a sewing needle, and when working with fine threads, it is easier to place gathering or pleating precisely.

Use an extremely strong fine yarn, such as a beading thread for gathering and pleating. If possible, use a color that matches or blends with the warp. Wind the length of auxiliary thread around a small bobbin or EZ-bob: you will need slightly more than the length to be gathered to allow for take-up and knotting. Tie a slipknot at the start and place the thread down between two warp threads. The auxiliary thread will be stitched up and down during weaving. I use a doubled thread so that I can tie the threads together at the end for greater security.

Hint: If the insertion is to be in the middle of a color block, use different-colored heddles on either side of the insertion point.

Weave at least two picks between the gathering stitches and at least eight picks between pleating stitches. You can vary the length of these stitches even within one piece.

When off the loom and before gathering or pleating, sew one end of the auxiliary thread neatly into the inkle (if using two threads, sew in one and then tie it securely to the other before sewing both neatly back and forth into a few picks). Then pull up the thread from the starting knot. Leave gathers in soft folds; shape pleats by finger pressing them along the folds.

Gathers and pleats with gathering threads near one side fall naturally into curves.

Reverses are not shown as they are the same as the front.

Center, Vertical

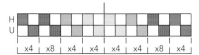

Red line marks position of gathering thread.

Warp: 2/16: navy, red violet, green, yellow

Weft: 2/16: navy

Gathering and pleating thread placed at center of the yellow strip.

A. Gathering over 4 and under 4 picks.

B. Pleating over 8 and under 8 picks.
Finger press folds to sharpen.

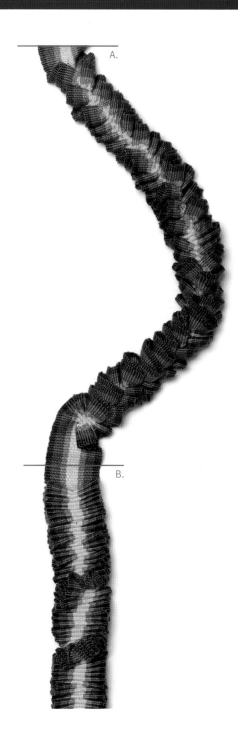

At One Side, Vertical

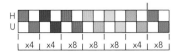

x4	x4	x8	x8	x8	x4	x8

Red line marks the position of the gathering thread.

Warp: 2/16: navy, purple, red violet, mauve, yellow, green.

Weft: 2/16: navy

A. Gathering vertically between green and blue stripes at right (see draft), all over 4, and progressively under 4, 6, 12, and 20 picks.

B. Pleating vertically between green and blue stripes at right (see draft), all over 4, and progressively under 4, 6, 12, and 20 picks.

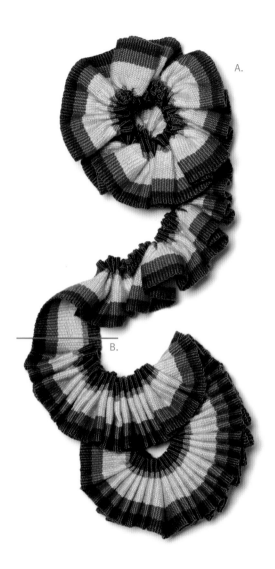

Scrunching and Shibori

Scrunching

Scrunching is done in exactly the same way as gathering or pleating, except that the auxiliary stitching thread moves diagonally to and fro across the warp.

Work inside a narrow edging. Starting at one side, stitch down and under, then up and over the selected number of picks and warp threads. You can vary the length and distance of the auxiliary stitches even within one piece.

The reverse is not shown as it is the same as the front.

Shibori

Traditionally, stitched shibori (a method of resist dyeing) is worked on a completed cloth, but inserting the gathering thread during weaving makes it much easier to place the stitches accurately. Using a white or pale warp is advisable for your first efforts, although working on carefully selected mixed colors can also be effective.

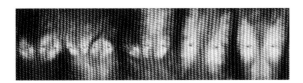

Vertical gathers can be made in the same way as described on page 130. Horizontal gathers can be made when the weft is inserted. Diagonal gathers can be made in the same way as for scrunching.

Try combining diagonal, vertical, and horizontal gathers as well as varying the length and position of the stitching as you weave. More than one auxiliary thread can be inserted at a time: diagonals worked in opposition are very effective.

After pulling up and securing the auxiliary thread, prepare and dye your piece as for the yarn used. Leave to dry completely. (It is tempting to peek, but resist!)

Carefully snip the auxiliary thread when dry and open out. Press if you wish. The holes where the auxiliary thread was positioned may show slightly, but this adds an extra dimension to the pattern. There will probably be slight bleeds of the dye, ranging from none when close to the drawn-in thread, to full dyeing on the completely exposed areas.

The reverse is shown where it differs from the front surface.

Scrunching and Shibori

Scrunching

Warp: 2/16, in colors indicated.
Repeat all color pairs x4.

Weft: 2/16, blue

Gathering, over 4 and under 4 picks, moving sideways over 8 warp threads each stitch.

Shibori

Warp: 2/16, cream

Weft: 2/16, cream

Zigzag gathering

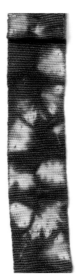

Diagonals with extra vertical stitches at side

Weft Manipulation

Dukagang

Dukagang is a Scandinavian technique using a supplementary pattern weft as an overlaid pattern thread on a solid-color plain-weave ground. The pattern weft is tied down to the ground fabric by inserting it under a single warp thread at regular intervals. A normal weft pick in between each overlay allows the same warp thread(s) to be used as tie-downs throughout. Often the fabric is woven facedown so that the short lengths of pattern thread linking or joining one row to the next are hidden beneath the cloth.

Applying Dukagang overlay to an inkle loom is quite easy. The pattern thread is tucked beneath the inkle as each row is finished and brought to the surface at the next required point.

Dukagang patterning is essentially composed of small squares; the length of the surface float between the tie-down warps determines how many rows are needed to make each pattern section square. The lengths of the floats between tie-downs is always the same. The pattern thread is thicker and is inserted only every alternate pick; a normal weft the same thickness as the warp weaves every pick.

When a row of squares has been woven, the pattern thread is carried by the shortest path up to the next overlaid row, usually on the underside of the inkle. It is also possible to make the links on the surface as well; in that case, it is sometimes necessary to adjust the number of overlays in a row to make the smallest possible join (see the face of section B, Dukagang Overlay 1, on page 136).

Method

Weave one pick with the normal weft.

Change the shed, beat, tug.

Insert the normal weft and keep the shed open.

Bring the pattern weft to the surface at the starting point for the overlay design; lay it across the inkle, passing it under the tie-down warp threads to the end of the design row; tuck the pattern thread below the inkle.

Change the shed, beat, tug.

Repeat this sequence, using the same floats and tie-downs until the required number of rows have been made to square the pattern. Then carry the pattern weft up to the start of the next sequence of rows as required.

Reverses

The reverses are not always neat, unless adjustments have been made to minimize the link.

When links are made on the surface, only narrow indented lines indicate where the tie-downs are. (See Section B, Dukagang Overlay 2, on page 136).

Design on squared paper, one square per block.

Dukagang Overlay

Warp: 2/16, medium blue

Weft: 2/16, medium blue

Pattern thread: 3x2/16, red or lemon.

Dukagang Overlay 1

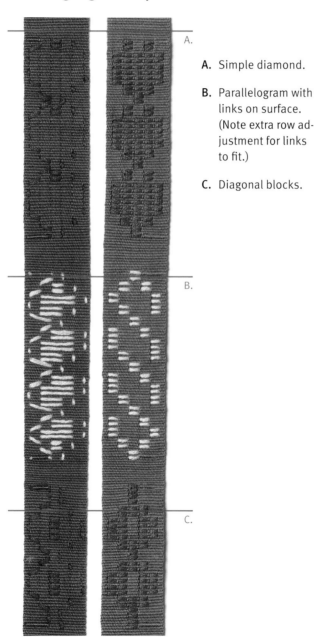

A.

B.

C.

A. Simple diamond.

B. Parallelogram with links on surface. (Note extra row adjustment for links to fit.)

C. Diagonal blocks.

Dukagang Overlay 2

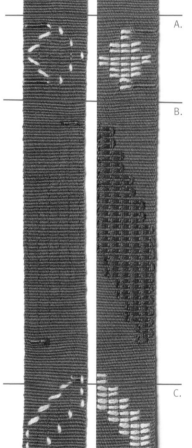

A.

B.

C.

A. Hearts.

B. Curved diagonals.

C. Chains.

Inlay

In contrast to overlaid patterns, such as Dukagang, the pattern weft in inlay lies in the same shed as the normal weft and is brought to the surface to float as required. The pattern thread becomes an additional weft that passes through the width of the inkle. However, if the pattern weft is taken from selvedge to selvedge, it will show at the edges. To prevent this, warp a vertical band of the same color as the pattern weft, but of the same thickness as the rest of the warp, and place it about three or four threads in from the edge on each side. The pattern weft is brought out of the shed just beyond these matching bands, passing to the next shed either below or above the inkle. The thicker pattern weft will make very small loops as it passes to the next pick. The normal weft goes from selvedge to selvedge throughout and is inserted in every pick.

Inlay on alternate picks

Change shed, beat, tug, weave normal weft from selvedge to selvedge.

Insert the pattern weft into the same shed, but only from vertical band to vertical band, bringing it to the surface as required for the pattern.

Change shed, beat, tug, weave normal weft.

Repeat.

Inlay in every pick

As above, but insert the pattern weft into every pick.

Two pattern wefts

Another form of inlay dispenses with the normal weft altogether and instead uses two different-colored pattern wefts, both inserted into every pick, and each brought to the surface where that color is required. By having two bands the same color as the pattern wefts at the sides, one pattern weft can weave from selvedge to selvedge, while the other turns at its own color. Always insert the selvedge-to-selvedge weft first.

In an even more specialized form of inlay, the whole surface is covered with pattern weft floats, each of which are separated by a single warp thread that prevents the directly adjacent pattern threads from seeming to overlap. Again, always insert the selvedge-to-selvedge weft first.

Beads

A prethreaded beading thread can also be inserted in any of these inlay techniques, either by bringing the beads to the surface between adjacent warp threads or by taking the beading thread over the number of warp threads required to place one or more beads on the surface. The beading thread can also be held over the inkle for a number of picks and reinserted either vertically or horizontally.

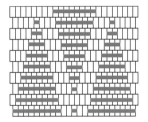

Designing

It is useful to design inlay on the basic indented pattern chart, although when working it is usually easy to see the position of the next float.

On the reverse, the design shows as a faint embossed pattern.

Single-Color Inlay

Pattern Thread in Alternate Picks

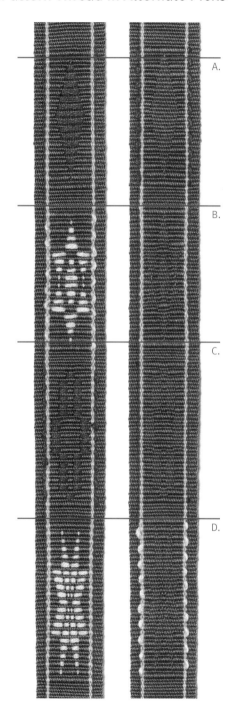

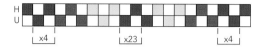

Warp: 2/16, medium blue, red, and yellow

Weft: 2/16, medium blue

Pattern weft: 3x2/16, red or lemon

A. Diamond: pattern weft turning below inkle.

B. Star: pattern weft turning above inkle.

C. Long curved shape: pattern weft turning above inkle.

D. Starburst: pattern weft turning below inkle.

Inlay

Pattern Thread in Every Pick

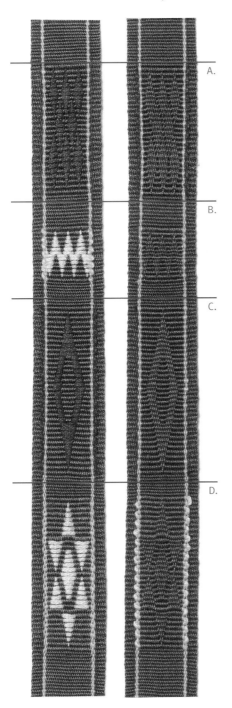

Warp: 2/16, medium blue, red, and yellow

Weft: 2/16, medium blue

Pattern weft: 3x2/16, red or lemon

A. Small diamonds: pattern weft turning below inkle.

B. Zigzag: pattern weft turning above inkle.

C. Shaped diamond: pattern weft turning above inkle.

D. Star 2: pattern weft turning below inkle.

Inlay with Two Pattern Wefts

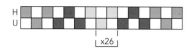

H
U
x26

Warp: 3x2/16, lemon, red, and blue

Pattern wefts: 3x2/16, red and blue, used together

Designs within Lemon Ground

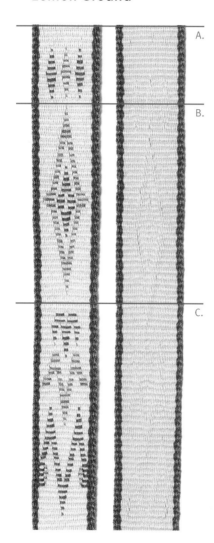

A.
B.
C.

A. Individual diamonds.

B. Diamond within diamond.

C. Zigzag shaping.

Designs Filling Whole Ground

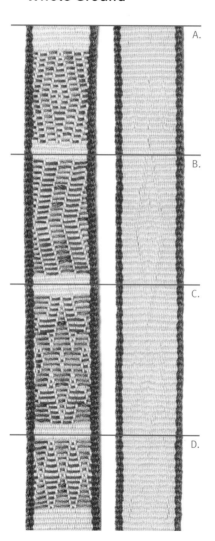

A.
B.
C.
D.

A. Framed diamond.

B. Diagonals.

C. Fancy pattern shapes.

D. Diamonds and triangles.

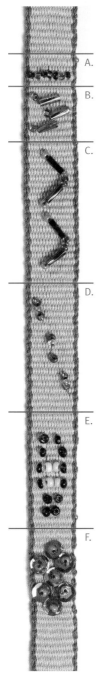

Beads on Inlay Weft

Warp: 2/16, purple and turquoise

Weft: 2/16, purple

Prethreaded beading weft

A. Rows.

B. Candles.

C. Swags: hold beading thread above surface until time to reinsert.

D. Diagonal groups: hold beading thread above the surface and reinsert at regular intervals.

E. Group: pull bead through between the warp ends.

F. Beads on sequins: beading thread through sequin, through bead, and back through sequin. Reinsert back into pick between same warp ends as it emerged.

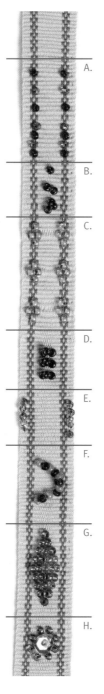

Border Pattern within Turquoise Ground

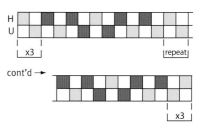

Warp: 2/16, purple and turquoise

Weft: 2/16, purple

Prethreaded beading weft

A. Beads in center of border patterns.

B. 1, 2, and 3 beads, reinserted where they emerged.

C. Groups of 4 within border.

D. Groups of 3 over 1 warp thread.

E. Beading weft turns above inkle just beyond border; bead covers the link.

F. Stitched swag: beading thread under a warp end at intervals so that the loop doesn't move.

G. Diamond: beads over 3 raised warp threads and under one.

H. Beads around sequin.

Selvedge Treatments

Beads

It is easiest to have beads on an unheddled beading thread (see pages 113–114), so the outer warp threads of this inkle are unheddled, with the beading thread placed alongside.

Secure the start of the beading thread before threading the beads onto it. Because beading thread is very slippery, the best method is to weave the start of the beading thread through the inkle together with the weft three or four times. Then thread the beads onto the beading thread in the order in which they will be required. Attach the beading thread to a light weight.

Hang the beading thread over the joining peg in the usual way (see pages 113–114). When a bead is required, bring it to the fell, then take the weft around the beading warp and above the bead before entering the next shed to lock the bead into position.

For beaded loops, leave the beading thread outside the weft, count the number of picks the loop is to span, then slide the beads down to the inkle, holding the loop in position so that the weft can enter the shed correctly.

TIP:

When the loop is on the open side of loom, hang the beading thread over the top peg where it will float before bringing the loop down.

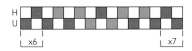

Warp: 2/16, mauve and turquoise

Weft: 2/16, mauve

For fringes or hanging lengths, the beads can be prethreaded or threaded as required, using a needle. When beads need to be manipulated on the beading thread (as when making picots, fringe, or clusters), the beading thread is re-threaded through a needle.

Beads 1

A. Beads on one edge only, placed every weft turn.

B. Beads on one side only, placed every other weft turn.

C. Using 2 separate beading threads, add beads on both edges, placing them every weft turn.

Beads 2

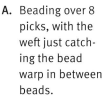
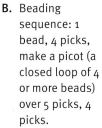
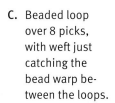
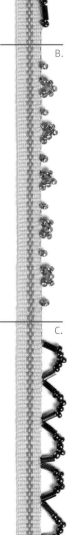

A. Beading over 8 picks, with the weft just catching the bead warp in between beads.

B. Beading sequence: 1 bead, 4 picks, make a picot (a closed loop of 4 or more beads) over 5 picks, 4 picks.

C. Beaded loop over 8 picks, with weft just catching the bead warp between the loops.

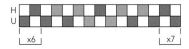

Warp: 2/16, mauve and turquoise

Weft: 2/16, mauve

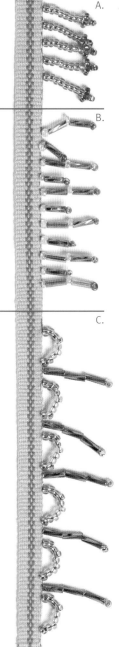

Beads 3

A. Beaded fringe with picot end: Stitch the bead warp through the number of beads for the length desired; add 3 beads at the end, then stitch back through the length, beginning with the fourth bead. Leave 2 weft picks between each fringe length.

B. Alternating short and long beaded fringe: Stitch through the length required; add 1 bead to hold, then stitch back through the long length. Leave 2 picks between each fringe length.

C. Beaded loop and fringe sequence: Loop over 6 picks; weave 2 picks, then make fringe desired length with a turning bead at the end. Leave 2 picks between repeats.

Beads 4

A. Beaded loops with an open cluster at base. Leave 2 picks between repeats. To make the cluster, gather several beads together at the turning end instead of just a single bead.

B. Bead with a drop-loop sequence: Place a single bead; weave 2 picks, make a loop using a bugle bead before the turning bead to form the drop. Weave 2 picks.

C. Beaded loop and cluster sequence: Use 2 beading warps. Make a loop using 1 warp, catching the base of the loop between 2 picks. Weave 6 picks, make a picot over 5 picks, using the second beading warp, weave 6 picks and fasten the loop of the first beading warp.

H
U   F
|x16|

Warp: 2/16 pink

F: the fancy yarn (unheddled)

Weft: 2/16, pink

Suspend the fancy yarns as described on page 123 or 130. The weft does not catch (or weave around) the unheddled fancy yarn every time.

Fancy Yarns, Single Side 1

A. Fancy yarn: soft, loose-twist yarn. Catch with weft to inkle every sixth pick (i.e., every third turn).

B. Fancy yarn: long chenille sections. Catch with weft every time, except in the chenille sections.

C. Fancy yarn: long chenille sections. Fold chenille sections to create picots as desired. Catch with weft every time.

Fancy Yarns, Single Side 2

A. Fancy yarn: marled black and cream with tufts. Catch every time except at the tufts.

B. Fancy yarn: super glitz. Catch on every eighth pick.

C. Fancy yarn: purple knots (commercial). Catch twice on consecutive turns in between knots.

Fancy Yarns

x16

Warp: 2/16, pink

F: Fancy yarns, unheddled, on both sides.

Weft: 2/16, pink

The weft does not catch (or weave around) the unheddled fancy yarns every time.

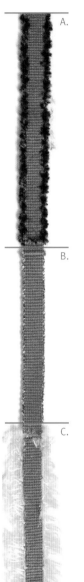

Fancy yarns, both sides 1

A.

B.

C.

A. Fancy yarn: chenille. Catch with weft to inkle every fourth pick.

B. Fancy yarn: glitz fingering. Catch with weft every turn.

C. Fancy yarn: soft fringed commercial yarn. Catch with weft to inkle every eighth pick.

Fancy yarns, both sides 2

A.

B.

C.

A. Fancy yarn: raffina (synthetic raffia). Catch with weft every sixth pick.

B. Fancy yarn: hand-knotted silk gimp. Catch with weft just before and just after knot, with 2 picks between.

C. Fancy yarn: 0.315mm wire. Catch with weft every turn. The inkle can be molded into waves after it is taken off the loom.

Clasped Wefts and Crossovers

It is usually preferable to use the same color weft as the selvedge threads of the inkle, unless there is a decorative reason; however, sometimes the two selvedges of the inkle need to be different colors.

In such cases, one color can be used as weft, and the weft will contrast at one selvedge, or a different color weft that contrasts with both sides can be used.

A third way, which allows both sides to have the correct color at the selvedges, is by clasping two wefts within the structure of the inkle.

Clasped warp ends have already been shown (see page 110). Clasping the weft is even simpler. Wind a ball of one of the weft colors and wind a shuttle with the other. Insert both wefts into the weaving in the usual manner for starting weaving, so that each yarn emerges from the correct selvedge for its color. Place the ball over the joining peg at one side of the inkle loom and rest it on the floor at the back. Insert the shuttle from the side, matching its color all the way through the shed; take the shuttle around the balled yarn and draw the shuttle back through the same shed to its own side, arranging the clasped join in the middle of the shed; change shed. Beat and tug both weft yarns as usual.

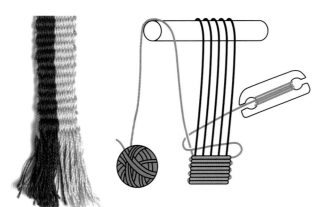

The yarn ball can be placed on whichever side suits you best.

Because clasped wefts are doubled in the shed, using a finer yarn for clasped wefts is best. Unfortunately, it is not always possible to obtain finer yarns to match the warp color, so the main samples on page 148 all have weft yarns the same thickness as those of the warp, which doubles the size of the weft and makes slightly wider wefts than usual.

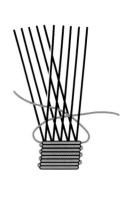

Crossovers

Making a plaited (braided) length in three colors is fun. Begin by weaving a short clasped weft section using two wefts that match the two outer warp colors, then make slits and weave three individual sections using matching weft colors. Add the matching weft for the center section and start and finish as usual. Finish with a short clasped weft section. Off the loom, plait (braid) the three separate lengths from top to bottom, untwisting and manipulating the joined part below where you are working through the slits to keep the plait flat. End the plait with the colors in the same places they were at the start. Manipulate and firm into shape.

When crossing over two wefts in the same pick, make an X with the wefts before bringing both down to the fell, changing the shed, and beating, to make sure that neither weft is above the other as they emerge from the shed.

Clasped Wefts and Crossovers

Clasped Wefts and Crossovers 1

Warp: 3x2/16, purple and gray

Weft: 3x2/16, colors as marked

A. Two clasped wefts: 3x2/16, purple and gray.

B. Two crossover wefts: 3x2/16, pink and purple.

C. Two crossover wefts: 3x2/16, gray and purple.

D. Two crossover wefts: 3x2/16, pink and deep mauve.

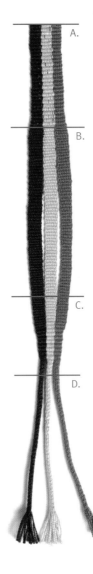

Clasped Wefts and Crossovers 2

Warp: 2/16, red violet, mauve, and purple

Weft: 2/16, colors as marked

A. Two wefts: 2/16, purple and red violet.

B. Slits: 3 wefts, 2/16, red-violet, mauve, and purple.

C. Joining section: 2 wefts, 2/16, purple and red violet.

D. Tubular: 3 wefts, 2/16, purple, mauve, and red violet.

Tablet-Woven Edging

Tablet weaving dates back to at least the fourth century BCE. The term cardweaving (not to be confused with card-loom weaving) is used in the United States because Mary Meigs Atwater translated the French terminology *tissage aux carton* as cardweaving, while at about the same time Mabel Peach in England translated the German *brettchenweberei* as tablet weaving.

Tablets (or cards) are hand-sized, flat, firm polygons with smooth holes at each corner. The most commonly used tablets are square, with 4 holes.

Warp threads are threaded through each corner hole. Turning one threaded tablet constantly in one direction will produce a 4-strand cord. If several tablets are placed side by side, each quarter turn of all the tablets can be held together with a single weft. The direction in which the tablets are turned can be reversed at will because the twist has been secured by the weft. Beyond the woven part, a reverse twist is also formed. If the tablets are always turned in one direction, eventually the twist will inhibit the use of the latter part of the warp. To counter this, in many traditional patterns the tablets are turned in sequences of rotation, for example, four turns in one direction followed by four turns in the reverse direction.

When tablets are used with an inkle loom, the tablets lie vertically at right angles to the weaver. The tablets can be threaded S or Z. Only two threads are shown in the following diagrams for clarity, but all threads in a single tablet must be threaded in the same direction.

Tablets can be turned forward (F, the top of the tablets turns away from the weaver) or backward (B, the top of the tablets turns toward the weaver).

Thread and warp each tablet separately on the inkle loom, following the pathway for an unheddled warp thread. Tie all four threads together at the starting peg. The weaving sequence is:

1. Turn tablet ¼ turn in the direction indicated.

2. Reach through tablet shed and change inkle shed.

3. Beat.

4. Tug.

5. Weave.

Tablet-woven selvedges produce neat corded edgings, which are a little thicker than the inkle. Use a weft that is the same as one of the colors in the outer tablet. A wider section of tablet weaving can also be inserted into the center of an inkle.

Many books are available about tablet weaving; they contain a wealth of patterns for further exploration.

Tablet-Woven Edging

x10

Warp: 3x2/16 purple
All tablets: 3x2/16
Weft: 3x2/16 purple
F = turn tablet forward
B = turn tablet backward

Tablets on One Edge

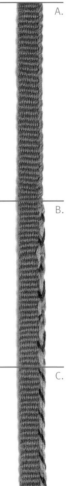

A.

B.

C.

All tablets threaded green and pink with the same colors in opposite holes.

A. One tablet, all green, threaded **S**.

Turns: all F.

B. Two tablets, four colors: purple, green, pink, turquoise; one threaded **Z** and one **S**.

Turns: 5xF, 5xB

C. Two tablets, four colors: purple, green, pink, turquoise; both threaded **Z**.

Second tablet turned ¼ turn F before starting.

Turns: all F.

Tablets on Two Edges

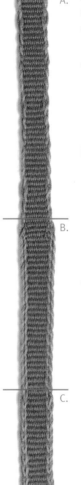

A.

B.

C.

All tablets threaded green and pink with the same colors in opposite holes.

A. One tablet at each edge threaded **Z** on left and **S** on right.

Turns: 8xF, 8xB.

B. Two tablets at each edge threaded **S** at left, **Z** at right.

Inner tablet turned ¼ turn B before starting.

Turns: all B.

C. Two tablets at each edge threaded **Z** then **S** on each side.

Turns: all F.

Inserted Fringe

Inserting a fringe from one side to the other of the inkle to make a fringe on both edges is not a stable method because the fringe can easily be pulled through the warp, so inserted fringes are only shown along one edge. For fringes on both sides, see page 154.

When inserting fringes, the weft weaves normally through every pick. The inserted fringe is added to it. Place the weft in the pick as usual before inserting the fringe length. It is easiest to have the fringe at the edge on the open side of the loom. Always take the weft *behind* any lengths of fringing.

The fringe can be made of a single strand or a group of several threads. It can match or contrast with the warp; more than one color can be used either in sequence or within groups. The fringe lengths can lie side by side as either single or double detached, or they can be inserted in rotation to make a decorative edging along the opposite edge. The fringe lengths can be all the same length or vary according to a predetermined pattern.

Working with cut lengths of fringe

To prepare cut lengths for fringing, wind yarn several times around two convenient pegs on the loom; cut through once. Long lengths can be halved after the initial cut.

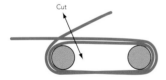

Detached single cut-length insertions

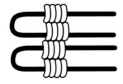

*Insert fringe from fringe side so that half the fringe length extends out the unfringed side.

Change shed, beat, tug, insert weft.

Fold the remaining fringe length and insert it through the shed to extend out the fringed side.

Change shed, beat, tug, insert weft.

Repeat from * as required.

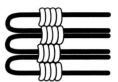

Detached double cut-length insertions

Insert fringe from fringe side so that half the fringe length extends out the other edge.

**Change shed, beat, tug, insert weft.

Fold the remaining fringe length and insert it through the shed to extend out the fringed edge.

In the *same shed*, add the next fringe length as you did the first.

Repeat from ** as required.

Cut-length insertions in rotation

Insert one fringe length so that its center is at the unfringed edge: change shed, beat, tug, insert weft.

Insert a *second fringe* length from the fringe edge as for the first.

Change shed, beat, tug, insert weft.

Fold the first fringe length and insert it into the shed to extend out the fringed edge; then, starting from the fringed edge, insert a new fringe length into the *same shed* so that half of it extends beyond the unfringed edge.

Change shed, beat, tug, insert weft.

Fold over the second fringe length and insert it through the shed to extend out the fringed edge.

Again insert another new fringe length into the *same shed*.

Change shed, beat, tug, insert weft.

Repeat as required.

Pull the fringe through the pick so that the loops lie close to the opposite edge.

Working with uncut fringe lengths

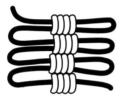

Uncut lengths of yarn can also be used for fringing. They can be either a single yarn or a group of yarns.

Two separate lengths of uncut fringe may also be worked in rotation.

The loops are all pulled through to emerge only on the fringed edge.

The loops of fringing can be cut afterward if required, or the loop can be worked around a template to produce the required size.

Inserted Fringe 1

Warp: 2/16 purple
Weft: 2/16 purple

Triple Rotation

A. Fringe: single strand of 3x2/16 in pink, blue, and green.

Insert individual colors in sequence every 3 picks.

Double Rotation

B. Fringe: single strand of 3x2/16 in purple and pale green.

One fringe color is always placed above the other at the unfringed edge.

Double Rotation, Loop Fringe

C. Fringe: single strands of 3x2/16 in deep and pale pink.

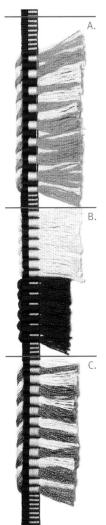

Inserted Fringe 2

Warp: 2/16, purple and cream
Weft: 2/16, purple

Double Rotation

A. Fringe: 3x(3x2/16) in pink and cream in every pick.

Detached Double Rotation in Repp

B. Fringe: 3x(3x2/16) in cream or purple to match upper warp color of the insertion shed.

Insert fringe into every alternate pick, matching upper warp color of the shed.

Double Rotation in Alternate Picks (Repp)

C. Fringe: 3x(3x2/16) in dark and pale green.

Inserted Fringe, Both Edges

Warp: 2/16 purple and mauve

Weft: 2/16 mauve

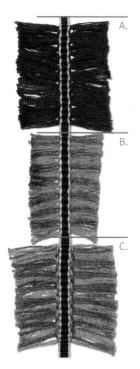

Inserted Fringe on Both Edges 1

Detached Single

A. Fringe: 3x(3x2/16), purple. Fringe turns worked at both edges.

Detached Double

B. Fringe: 2x(3x2/16), green and blue. Fringe turns worked at edges.

Rotation

C. Fringe: 2x(3x2/16), red violet and light rose. Fringe turns worked at edges.

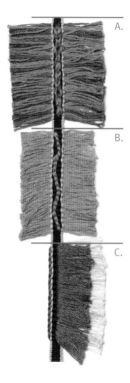

Inserted Fringe on Both Edges 2

Variable rotation

A. Fringe: 2x(3x2/16), red violet and blue. Fringe turns worked at center.

Detached Double

B. Fringe: 2x(3x2/16), red violet. Fringe turns worked at variable places at center.

Rotation

C. Fringe: 2x(3x2/16), dark green on top row, pale green on lower row. Turns on top row worked from side to center and turns on lower row from center to edge.

Inserted Fringes along Both Edges

Although inserted fringe should always be placed along only one side for stability, two different sets of fringe can be inserted from both sides simultaneously to produce fringe along both edges. Insert in the usual way, placing two fringe lengths, one from each side together in the same shed opening. Warning: When working double-detached or rotation-inserted fringes, do not use fringe that is too bulky because twice as many fringe threads pass through each pick as when it is worked along only one edge.

Double Rows of Fringing

Fringes can be worked in two or more rows. When making rows of inserted fringes, the fringe lengths must fill the entire pick, with the turns of the fringes emerging somewhere within the width of the inkle. The fringes can overlap each other if required.

Knotted Fringe

Knotted fringes are easiest when made with precut lengths—make sure they are long enough to manipulate. Again they can be single strands or multiples. Because they are secure they can be worked on both sides of the inkle.

Working on a closed shed

Knotted fringes worked with the shed closed can be made around single warp ends or around two or more ends, with the loop placed either on top or underneath at the selvedge. Because they are worked on a closed shed, these knots are visible on both sides of the band.

Start with the shuttle on the unfringed edge and weave 2 partial picks across and back, leaving the warp thread(s) unwoven where the knot will be made.

With the shed closed, knot the fringe around the unwoven warp ends.

Weave 2 full picks before making the next knot.

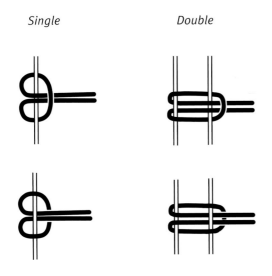

Single   Double

Working on an open shed

When knots are worked around the warp ends with the shed open, the underside of the knot lies within the weaving and cannot be seen on the underside of the inkle. As a result, knots worked on an open shed can

be placed anywhere on the inkle and need not always be at the edges. Both single and double knots can be made.

Insert weft as normal, then knot the fringe around desired ends in the top layer of the shed.

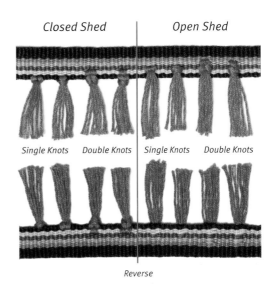

Closed Shed   *Open Shed*

Single Knots   Double Knots   Single Knots   Double Knots

Reverse

Finishing all types of knotted fringe

Make sure all the lengths are secured in position after the weaving is finished. Comb or brush the fringe length, trimming off any overlong fringes.

If you wish to vary the shape of the base of the fringe, cut out the design on paper first, making several copies if your inkle is longer than the sheet. On the back of the sheet, mark a line where the edge of the inkle will lie and stick a length of double-sided tape below the shape. Pin or secure the inkle along the line marker at the back, remove the top cover of the sticky tape, and neatly place the fringe onto the tape. Cut along the shape.

Knotted Fringe, One Edge

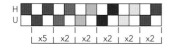

Warp: 3x2/16, purple, red violet, light rose, medium purple, mauve

Weft: 3x2/16, purple

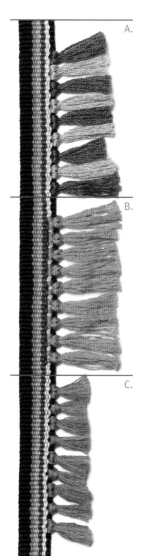

Knotted Fringe 1

A. Fringe: 4x(3x2/16), alternating light rose, medium purple, all the same length.

Single knot with loop underneath worked over 4 warp ends on a closed shed.

Two weft picks between knots.

B. Fringe: 4x(3x2/16) in red violet, all the same length.

Double knot with loop underneath worked over a total of 8 warp ends on a closed shed.

Two weft picks between knots.

C. Fringe: 4x(3x2/16), two each green and turquoise, all the same length.

Single knot, alternating loop over and loop under, worked over 4 warp ends on a closed shed. Two weft picks between knots.

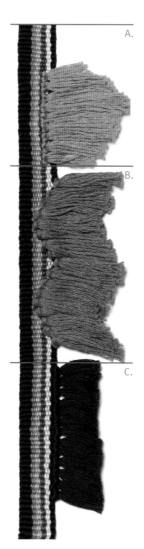

Knotted Fringe 2

A. Fringe: 4x(3x2/16), red violet, cut to shape after weaving.

Single knot, with loop underneath, worked over 2 warp ends on an open shed, every second pick.

B. Fringe: 4x(3x2/16), in green, all same length.

Single knot on an open shed, loop over, worked over 2 warp ends every second pick. Knots positioned in waves moving from one edge to the center and back.

C. Fringe: 4x(3x2/16) in purple, all the same length.

Single knot, loop under, worked over 2 warp ends on an open shed every second pick along the edge.

Warp: 3x2/16, purple and mauve

Weft: 3x2/16, purple

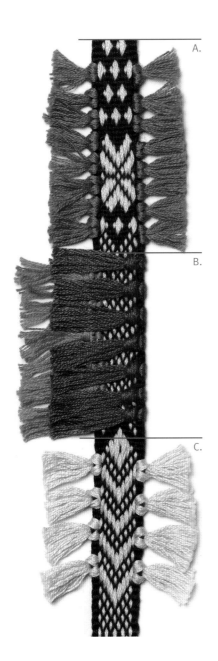

Closed Shed Knotted Fringe on a Baltic-Style Pattern

A. Fringe: 4x(3x2/16), green.

Single knot with loop under, alternately knotted at each side.

B. Fringe: 4x(3x2/16), medium purple and blue.

Double knot with loop over, alternately knotted at each side, but both arranged to face the same way.

C. Fringe: 8x(3x2/16), mauve.

Single knot with loop under, spaced to fit with pattern.

Knotted Fringe, Two Edges

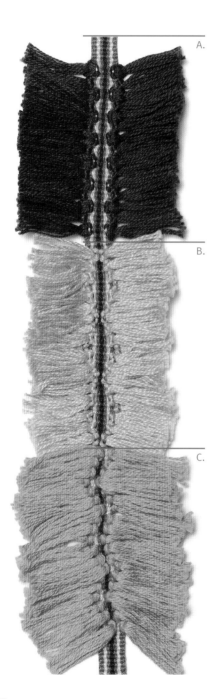

Warp: 2/16, red violet, light rose, medium purple, purple

Weft: 2/16, red violet, as edge of inkle

Open Shed Knotted Fringe

A. Fringe: 2x(3x2/16), purple.

Alternating single and double knots with loops underneath on alternate picks, placed along edge only.

B. Fringe: 2x(3x2/16), light rose.

Single knots with loops under, placed on alternate picks in curves from middle to edge and back.

C. Fringe: 2x(3x2/16), red violet.

Single knots, with loops under, placed on alternate pick in sinuous lines.

Manipulating the Width of the Inkle

Control of the Width by the Weft Tensioning

An inkle can be adjusted in width by simply drawing the weft tighter or looser. There is a maximum width, over which the weft will begin to show, and also a minimum width, when the weft cannot be pulled any tighter. When the weft is pulled in to its limit, any patterning will become distorted. Between these two extremes, however, a great deal of variation is possible.

Decreasing the Number of Warp Threads

Warp threads can be discarded during weaving to reduce the width of the inkle. You can discard either from the edges, or from the middle. If the ratio of warp discards to picks is 2:1 (2 warp ends discarded per pick), then narrowing will occur more quickly, making a shallower angle and a shorter-length triangle. When only 1 warp end is discarded per pick (one side for 1 pick and the other for the next for a 1:1 ratio) or when 2 warps (one on each side) are discarded on 1 pick and then a pick woven without discarding—a 2:2 ratio—the decrease occurs more gradually, producing a longer, steeper angle. Discards can also be made on one side only, when the ratio will be 1:1 (1 warp end discarded per pick) for a shallow angle and 1:2 (1 warp end discarded every 2 picks) for a steep one.

Discarding from the edges

If discarding from the edges, cut out one thread at a time, making the cut at some distance from the fell. You can leave the cut threads hanging until the inkle is removed from the loom. Discarded threads can either be left as they are to form a fringe at the sides (they will be quite secure), or the ends can be stitched through a pick in the inkle to the opposite edge. Alternately, cut warp ends can be placed through the next pick together with the weft; ends that are very close

to the edge may need to be woven or stitched through two consecutive picks before they are cut. Uncut lengths of warp ends can also be used to make cords, tassels, or braids along the edges.

The advantage of discarding from the edges is that the tabby structure is always maintained. The disadvantage is that the weft will inevitably show at the edges in patterned inkles, once the border matching the weft is gone.

Discarding from within the inkle or from the center

When discarding from within the inkle, 2 warp threads need to be discarded together to maintain the tabby structure.

However, if discards are made beginning at the center of a symmetrical pattern, you can remove the first one from the center by itself and then discard two at a time to keep the symmetry. The doubled warp threads at the center will only be there for a short time. Unless the discarded threads are to be inserted into the next pick together with the weft, it is easiest to keep the discarded threads above the inkle until after the inkle is finished and removed from the loom.

Discards from the center can either be stitched individually through a pick to the edge or corded, tasseled, or braided to lie on top of the inkle. Those taken to the edges can be cut close to the edge. Again, ends that are very close to the edge may need to be woven or stitched through 2 consecutive picks before they are trimmed, or braided, or finished in groups.

The advantage of discarding from within the width of the inkle is that you can control the position of the discarded warps because they can occur at any point across the inkle. This allows edge patterns, for instance, to frame the inkle right to the finish so the weft does not show. The disadvantage is that sometimes a true tabby structure cannot be maintained.

Increasing the Number of Warp Threads

Warp threads can also be added to an existing warp. If you're starting with a narrow point, place a minimum of 4 or 5 warp threads on the loom for the secure start. To add warp threads, it can be easier to take the new thread from the starting peg backward along the warp pathway. Place unheddled threads under the top peg and tie to the start.

Heddled threads need to be placed over the top peg and then through a heddle before tying them to the start. To position the heddle, place a doubled heddle under the heddle peg (with knots underneath), thread the warp thread through both loops, then tie it to the start. Loose warp ends can be stitched into the inkle, or corded, tasselled, or braided as described above.

Adding threads to the edges

To add threads on the edges, tie in a new warp length either on every side per pick for a ratio of 2:1 (2 warps increased per pick) for a shallower angle or on every other side per pick (1 warp increased per pick) for a 1:1 ratio and a steeper angle.

The advantage of adding threads to the edges is that it is easier than adding warp thread in the center because the position of the new warp thread is clear. The disadvantage is that when using several different colors in a pattern, the weft thread will show at the selvedges unless the added warps are the same color as the weft.

Adding threads within the width of the inkle

To add threads to an existing symmetrical pattern or to start a new one, add two adjacent threads (either both heddled or both unheddled) together with a final single thread to maintain the symmetry. If complete symmetry is not required, then a heddled and an unheddled thread can be inserted together. If adding threads to two symmetrical patterns at once, adjust the ratio to suit.

The advantages of adding threads within the width of the inkle are that patterns can be inserted or continued exactly as required, and the weft does not show at the edges. The disadvantage is that it is extremely fiddly to insert new warp threads between the existing ones.

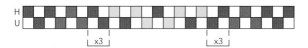

Warp: 3x2/16, purple, red, yellow

Weft: 3x2/16, purple

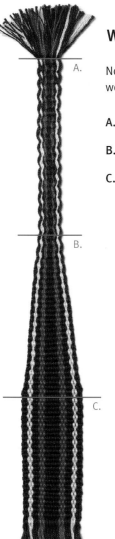

Weft Tensioning

Note: Techniques on this band are worked from the bottom upward.

A. Weft pulled in tightly.

B. Loosening tension.

C. Maximum width for this inkle. Increasing and decreasing at the edges.

Increasing and Decreasing at Edges

Note: Techniques on this band are worked from the bottom upward.

A. Decreasing warps, by 1 end per pick (1:1 ratio).

Groups of 4 discarded warp threads knotted at edges.

B. Increasing warp threads by 2 ends per pick (2:1 ratio).

Warp ends stitched through picks at back.

Starting fringe whipped with existing thread.

Manipulating Width

Warp: 3x2/16, purple, red, yellow

Weft: 3x2/16, purple

A.

B.

Increasing and Decreasing Direct from Center

Note: Techniques on this band are worked from the bottom upward.

A. Decreasing by 2 warp ends every 2 picks at center (2:2 ratio).

Discarded warp threads braided into 4-strand round braids at center above inkle.

B. Increasing by 2 warp ends per pick at center (2:1 ratio).

Warp ends stitched through back of pick to edges and left as fringe.

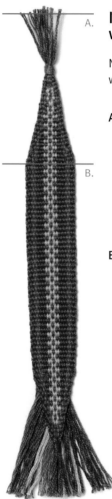

A.

B.

Increasing and Decreasing within Inkle

Note: Techniques on this band are worked from the bottom upward.

A. Decreasing by 2 every second pick at various points within inkle (2:2 ratio), without disrupting the center motif.

Discarded warp threads stitched through back of picks and cut close to edges.

B. Increasing by 2 warp ends per pick at various points within inkle (2:1 ratio), starting with edge, and then center motif.

Warp ends stitched through to back of inkle in place where inserted and left as fringe.

Finishings

Before you start to warp your inkle band, you need to consider how it will be finished. If long fringing is required, extra warp length needs to be allowed at the beginning and end of the weaving.

The secure start and finish outlined on page 14 is sufficient for a neat flat finish or for turning a hem at the end. If you want extra long fringes, however, you have many choices.

Simple Tassels

The end of the inkle can be drawn up by tightening the tail of weft left at both start and finish. Stitch the tail through the inkle to secure it, or use the tightened weft yarn to bind the head of the tassel, or whip (wrap) with a separate thread. (See below.)

To make tassels with neatly trimmed ends, wrap a short length of paper tightly around the tassel threads and cut through everything at the length you require. The tassel threads will then all be the same length.

Slipknots (or Thumb Knots)

If you want to divide the warp ends into smaller sections while working, it is useful to lightly tie the individual bundles into a small slipknot. With all the threads together, wrap the shorter end around finger and thumb of one hand to make a loop; from the back, push a short loop up between the main loop, leaving a tail at the back, and tighten the main loop. To release the knot, simply tug on the loose end.

An extended version of the slipknot, used for temporarily joining two threads, is to tie a single half knot, then make a slipknot above it with one end over the other end, again leaving a tail before tightening.

Woven Fringes

For woven fringes, divide the warp into sections and weave each section separately, either flat or as a tube.

Braided and Plied (Corded) Fringes

When planning for braided or plied fringe, make sure to allow extra length because not only is the take-up considerable, but you will also need extra length to manipulate the braid.

Braids can be flat or rounded and can be worked with single threads or several threads together.

The simplest of the flat braids is the 3-strand braid. Divide the bundle of warp threads into three groups; working alternately from the right and then left, pass the outer group over the middle one to the center. For a very neat, firm braid, make a 5-strand braid. Pass the outer group over two groups to the middle, again working alternately from right and left and making sure to keep the groups in order.

The advantage of round braids is that it doesn't matter which way they lie. The 4-strand round braid is probably one of the most useful. Divide a section of warp threads into four groups; working alternately from right and then left, take the outer group from one side under two groups, bring to the surface, and take the same group back over one group, so that it remains on the same side as it started (although now inside the other group of threads from that side). Repeat, working from alternate sides.

Plied cords can be worked with as few as two threads. Divide a section of warp into two, overtwist each group separately in the same direction, then place the two groups together and, still controlling them, allow them to twist back around each other in the opposite direction. Secure the ends. Plied cords can also be made by twisting more than two groups together.

Overhand Knots

Separate groups of warp threads can be tied close to the woven section; a simple overhand knot is sufficient. They can also be used to secure the ends of braids or cords.

Securing the Ends of Braids and Cords

In addition to overhand knots, the ends of braids and cords can also be secured by wrapping (also called whipping or binding), either with existing threads from the fringe or with a separate length of thread.

Wrapping with an existing thread from the fringe can be worked either upward or downward. Your fringe will need extra length for this technique.

To wrap upward, place a loop of separate yarn along the fringe with the loop upward toward the inkle. Wrap a thread from the end of the braid, cord, or tassel tightly and closely upward around both the tassel and loop five or six times. Insert the very end of the whipping thread through the loop and pull the ends of the loop to bring the whipping thread through the wrapping to become part of the tassel.

To wrap downward: Starting at the top, use one of the threads from the fringe to wrap tightly downward around all the other threads. To secure the wrapping, stitch the end of the binding thread upward through the binding, across the head of the tassel, and downward through the binding.

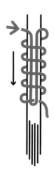

Using a separate thread for whipping is useful if you want the binding to contrast with the tassel. Make a loop at one end of the whipping thread and place it against the tassel with the loop pointing downward away from the inkle. Carefully hold the beginning of the whipping thread and loop with one hand, use the other hand to wrap the long end of the whipping thread tightly and closely downward several times. Place the end of the whipping thread through the loop at the bottom and using the short tail at the top, draw the loop up through the wrapping until the clasped part of the whipping thread lies inside the wrapping. Pull both ends firmly, one up and one down, to tighten the whipping, then snip the extra whipping threads close to the whipping.

Stitching Inkles Together

Place the inkles side by side. Safety pins placed at intervals can help to keep the inkles aligned for sewing. Use the same thread as the outer edge of the warp, and stitch through the turns of the weft threads. If you plan your inkle with a wide plain border on one side and a narrow one on the other, then joining wide to narrow will help to disguise the join.

Warp Draft Threading Charts

The shaded squares or rectangles show where the warp threads go.

Normal threads are shown as squares; thicker or double threads as rectangles.

Basic Threading Chart

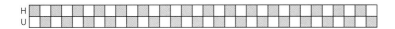

Use for warp-color patterns, pick-up, lettering, additions to warp surface, and basic weft manipulation.

Mark repeats according to your pattern.

Krokbragd Threading Chart

Add edging threads as for normal tabby (H/U2 only).

Warp drafts with thicker pattern threads.

The darker shaded rectangles are the pattern threads; the lighter squares the background.

Repeat the units as often as required. Add border designs at the sides to suit.

Baltic-Style Threading Chart

(Pattern threads are either a single thicker thread or doubled normal threads.) Add one extra pattern thread at the end.

Monk's Belt Threading Chart

South American Pebble Threading Chart

Add one heddled thin thread after the repeats.

Pattern Charts for Designing

Basic Warp-Color Pattern Chart

Use for basic warp-color patterns and inlay.

Pick-up Pattern Chart

Use for unheddled and/or heddled pick-up.

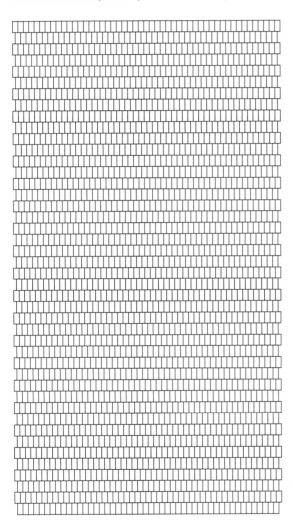

Lettering Pattern Chart

Mark width to suit. Use for compensating lettering and two-thread inlay.

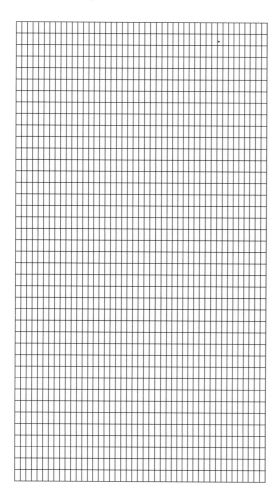

Baltic-Style Pattern Charts
(for 5, 9, and 13 pattern threads)

South American Pebble Pattern Chart

Mark width to suit.

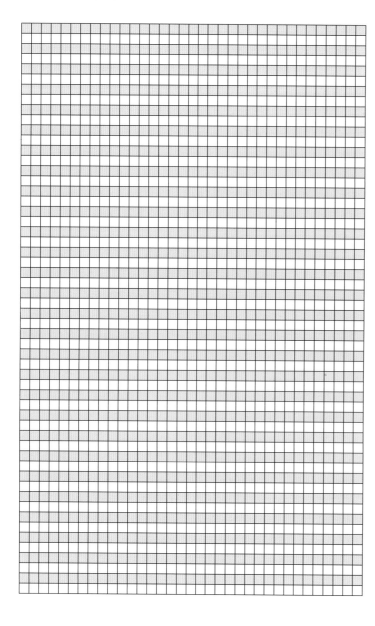

Glossary

Balanced weave: A woven structure in which both warp and weft show equally.

Basketweave: A woven structure in which two warp and/or two weft threads work together side by side.

Beat: The firm pushing of the weft thread into position in the warp.

Beater: A thin implement used to push the weft in the previous shed firmly into place.

Binding: *see* Wrapping.

Braces (Suspenders): Fabric or leather straps worn over the shoulders to hold up trousers. Inkles, especially Baltic-style and other figured inkles, have traditionally been used for this purpose. Braces is British English usage; suspenders, American English.

Braid: The interlacement or intertwining of three or more strands, in which all the strands are used in turn, with no separate weft.

Count: A numerical indication of the thickness of the yarn.

Draft: A chart that denotes the order in which the warp threads are to be placed on the loom.

End: A single warp thread.

e.p.cm (ends per centimeter): The metric equivalent of e.p.i.

e.p.i. (ends per inch): The number of warp threads per inch.

Fell: The position of the last pick of weft.

Flap: A pivoting block.

Float: A warp or weft thread that does not interlace in tabby order and rises above the background, usually for a decorative effect.

Heading: A short piece woven before and after the main weaving, often of waste yarn.

Heald: *see* Heddle.

Heddle: A loop into which selected warp ends are threaded to be able to create an automatic shed. Also called leash or heald.

Leash: *see* Heddle.

Loom: Any structure than holds warp threads taut for weaving.

Pattern chart: The graph on which the structure of the design is diagrammed.

Peg (on an inkle loom): Short horizontal bars that lie at right angles to the inkle loom and around which the warp is wrapped.

Pick: A single row of inserted weft.

Plain weave: *see* Tabby.

Plait: *see* Braid.

Plied cord: Two or more strands or groups of yarn twisted together to make one narrow structure. Can be twisted S or Z.

Ply: The twisting together of two or more strands or groups of threads.

Repp: Alternating picks of thick and thin weft.

Row: *see* Pick.

Selvedges: The outer edges where the weft turns and encloses the woven structure.

Sett: The number of warp ends in a single unit of measurement.

Shed: The opening between the raised and lowered warp ends into which the weft is placed.

Shuttle: A stick or other implement for holding the weft thread.

Stitch: Used to denote the vertical length of a warp float in pick-up patterns.

Suspenders: *see* Braces.

Tabby: A weave structure in which both warp and weft repeatedly pass over one thread and under the next.

Take-up: The reduction in the original warp length caused by the interlacement of the warp with the weft.

Tassel: Several loose threads wrapped, whipped, or bound together.

Tension: The degree to which the warp is stretched during weaving.

Tensioning device: A mechanism on the inkle loom to adjust the tension of the warp.

Swivel block: *see* Flap.

Sliding peg: A peg on the inkle loom that can be fixed into position within a groove.

Warp: The threads that are placed on the loom.

Warp-faced: A weave structure where the warp ends lie closely together, and the weft is hidden.

Weft: The thread that is placed between selected warp ends.

Weft-faced: A weave structure where the weft threads lie closely together, and the warp is hidden.

Whipping: *see* Wrapping.

Woven: A structure where selected warp ends are lifted, and the weft is placed under these ends and over the dormant ends.

Wrapping: Wrapping one of the threads in a group of threads around all the threads several times to bind or secure them.

Yarn: Any type of thread that can be used for weaving.

Yarns

Note

20/2 pearl cotton is a good substitute for 2/16 cotton.

5/2 pearl cotton is an excellent substitute for 3x2/16 yarns.

U.S. Retailers

The Lone Star Loom Room

1146 Gardencrest Ln.

Houston, TX 77077

(888) 562-7012

lonestarloomroom.com

The Lunatic Fringe

1447 Deer Run Rd.

Havana, FL 32333

(800) 483-8749

lunaticfringeyarns.com

UKI

ukisupreme.com

Outside the United States

The Handweavers Studio and Gallery

140 Seven Sisters Rd.

London, United Kingdom N7 7NS

handweavers.co.uk

Inkle Looms

U.S. Retailers

Halcyon Yarn

12 School St.

Bath, ME 04530

(800) 341-0282

(207) 442-7909

halcyonyarn.com

Schacht Spindle Company

6101 Ben Pl.

Boulder, CO 80301

(303) 442-3212

(303) 447-9273

schachtspindle.com

Webs

75 Service Center Rd.

Northampton, MA 01060

(800) 367-9327

yarn.com

The Yarn Barn of Kansas

930 Massachusetts St.

Lawrence, KS 66044

Sales: (800) 468-0035

yarnbarn-ks.com

Outside the United States

Ashford Handicrafts

ashford.co.nz

The Handweavers Studio and Gallery

140 Seven Sisters Rd.

London, United Kingdom N7 7NS

handweavers.co.uk

George Weil

Old Portsmouth Rd.

Peasmarsh, Guildford

United Kingdom GU3 1LZ

georgeweil.com

LeClerc Looms

1573 Savoie

PO Box 4

Plessisville, QC

Canada G6L 2Y6

leclerclooms.com

Organizations

The Association of Guilds of Weavers, Spinners, and Dyers

The umbrella group for the many U.K. guilds, including an online Guild. The *Journal* is a quarterly publication of the Association.

wsd.org.uk

The Braid Society

Informative quarterly members' newsletter and an annual publication, *Strands*.

braidsociety.com

Handweavers Guild of America

weavespindye.org

Index

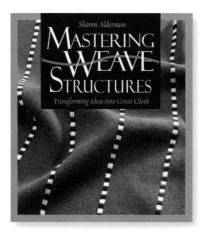